The Secret To Getting Through Life's Difficult Changes

By Lillie R. Brock & Mary Ann Salerno

Washington, D.C.

Durban, South Africa

Published by: Bridge Builder Media

This 3rd Edition published 1998

INTERCHANGE INTERNATIONAL INC.
1001 G Street, NW, Suite 200 East
Washington, DC 20001-4545
202..783..7700 800..878..8422
fax: 202..783..7730
email: changecycl@aol.com
website: www.changecycle.com

Library of Congress Catalog Card Number 93-73879

ISBN 0-9638959-0-7

Cover Design: Marcia Delong
DeLong Lithographics, Lorton, Virginia
Vicky White and Victoria Light
White Light Publishing, Huntington
Beach California

Typography & Production: Jim Wrightsman
MARVIN SERVICES CORPORATION, Dallas, TX

Dedication

For my Mother, Joan,
with love and gratitude, admiration and respect.
—Mary Ann

For Mom and Daddy,
whose unmatched love has always made it safe for me to change.
—Lillie

Acknowledgements

Most of all, to God who is the true source of the Change Cycle™. We are humbled and grateful that You entrusted us with this life changing tool.

A heartfelt *Thank You* to Arly for her guidance and caring about us, this book and our work with the Change Cycle™. We love you neighbor!

To Pam Pryor, with love and gratitude for her personal and professional encouragement, perseverance, humor and assistance through it all.

We are very grateful for the editorial expertise of Marcia Broucek. A million thanks to Susan Wray for deciphering our handwriting and getting the text into the computer, and Susan Greene for copy-editing and other miracles. A special blessing to Jim Wrightsman for his text design and editing, as well as his gentle insistence for us to use technology now.

We never could have done it without the insights and suggestions of Marjory Zoet Bankson, Julie Beckman, Linda Brock, Thom Bunce, Anna Hebner, Sandy Menefee, Suzanne Schmidt, Coni Staff and Nancy Tolbert. Thank you, again and again.

To Milton Aschner of Ussery Printing for his advice and expertise in printing and design, you have been a dear friend and tremendous help. To Marcia DeLong of DeLong Lithographers, Julie Stanish of A-Stanishing

Productions and to Vicky White and Victoria Light at White Light Publishing. your talents and artistic achievements are recognized and appreciated.

To our colleague, Robyn Sandy in Durban, South Africa, we salute your commitment to positive change; in your life, in your business and in your country.

With tremendous respect and appreciation, we thank Dr. Phillip Zimbardo of Stanford University, Dr. David Allen of the Minirth-Meier & Bryd Clinic and Julie Silverthorn and John Overdurf of Neuro-Energetics Inc. Your expertise around the psychology of change assisted us in communicating the form and function of the Change Cycle™.

For our Change Cycle Locator™ partners, Denny Coates and Meredith Bell of Performance Support Systems Inc., we appreciate your belief in us and all that's yet to be.

We could never express the importance of the love and support of our family and friends. Your encouragement and belief in us through all the years brings both a tear and a smile.

To all of the *Successful Changers* who have inspired our work, we are forever grateful.

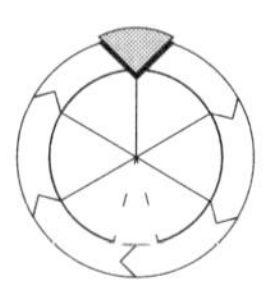

Table of Contents

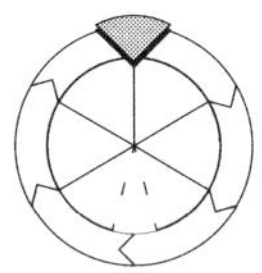

Introduction

In the spring of 1992, as I unpacked some old boxes in my new office, I came across an unlabeled file with a single sheet of paper in it. On that piece of paper, years before, I had drawn a crude circle and written five words around the edge. It was if I was taking dictation because I wrote as fast as I could without thought. When I finished, I stared at the words and knew I did not yet understand their impact. I put the paper in a file folder and then into my desk drawer. I never gave it another thought, so when I happened on it, I felt a sense of discovery.

As Mary Ann and I studied it, we knew that it was a treasure map of sorts. We felt it described what we had experienced ourselves and seen others go through in changing situations, personally or at work. We decided that, at the very least, we would clean it up, name it the Change Cycle™ and use it as a teaching tool in our trainings.

In August of 1992, we traveled to Johannesburg, South Africa, where I delivered a keynote address to the 325 delegates of the National Working Women's Convention. Additionally, we did several other training programs around South Africa, the final one for ESCOM, the electric company of Africa. The night before the training, as we met with the company representative, we were briefed on the general attitude of the employees and what had been going on at this power station. The picture she painted was bleak. The employees were angry, discontented, and distrusting because of the way management was handling a major restructuring. Suddenly, I felt very nervous and apprehensive about what I was about to face. Deep inside I knew that what I had prepared to train was not what they needed.

After tossing and turning for hours, I got out of bed about 4:30 a.m. and sat down with the Change Cycle™ and a legal pad. I prayed that God would give me some insight about what I should do and say in the training. After about ten minutes, I began to write. Again, as before, I had no idea what I was writing and when finished, I had written more of the words you now see on the completed Change Cycle™. I felt certain that God had given me those words and at 8 a.m., I stood up in front of those people and talked about the Change Cycle™ for three hours, as though I had done it many times. Mary Ann stood in the back of the room and just shook her head. Everyone responded very positively and we have since been asked to return.

We could hardly wait to sit down and talk about what had happened and what had been entrusted to us. We knew that it was an important and powerful tool even in it's original crude form. We were excited about the opportunity to refine the language and do the research to prove the Change Cycle's meaning. We were confident that, since God had given it, proving its validity would be easy. As you would know, it has been.

So, we both offer you this book, hoping that it will teach you as much as it has taught us. We are humbled by the way the Change Cycle™ began and we are confident that these pages offer the proof and insight to its profound message. As you read, allow yourself to experience what it would be like to be in control of the changes in your life.

We believe that the motivation and power exists within you to use change as a catalyst to create the life you desire. Tapping into that power is the secret. Channeling that power takes you to where the answers and rewards are. Oh yes, and always remember, a little change can change a lot.

Lillie — Mary Ann

Lillie R. Brock — *Mary Ann Salerno*

"It is not the strongest of the species that survives, nor the most intelligent, but rather the one most responsive to change."

Charles Darwin

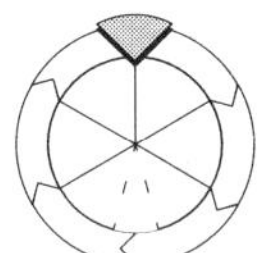

Chapter 1

Change: Good or Bad?

Red and Winnie were devoted to each other and still very much in love when death took her from him. They had been married 57 years and Red's heart had a loneliness that words could never express.

To be near his son and granddaughter, Red moved from his home to Orlando. Healthy, but miserable, surrounded by a loving family and new friends, but painfully alone, he sat day after day and watched the moments pass by. The changes in his life had left him with losses he could hardly bear and yet the sun came up every morning and forced him to go on. They say time takes care of everything and, in its own way, it took care of Red. His anger and bitterness softened to despair and somewhere inside his heart called out to be thankful for what was, by remembering what had been. He began to take inventory of his life through his memories and cycled through the laughter, joys, and tears of his youth, his family, his work, and his friendships. These memories stirred in him the longing to reconnect with his past.

The people, the places, the events of the previous years all came together and landed on the memory of Myrtle. It had been sixty years since he'd dated that Southern Georgia woman. He had no idea if she had moved away, married, or was even still alive. He wrote a note to the Cairo, Georgia, newspaper asking if they knew of her whereabouts and if so, requested that they send on his address and phone number. That letter arrived on the desk of the Editor of *The Cairo Messenger*. He read with a smile Red's request and was so pleased to be able to deliver the note himself to Ms. Myrtle who, at 82 years old, still worked across the street as the Secretary to the President of the Rodenberry Pickle Company.

Myrtle, you might say, was quite surprised to be hearing from Red after all these years. Her phone call rekindled in him the desire to be alive, to have a life again. She invited him to visit and, within one week, his hair cut and car waxed, he was on his way. They enjoyed each other immensely and began to "date" again. Cards, phone calls, and frequent visits over only a couple of months led these two right down the aisle. Red puts his latest view of marriage very simply, "When you are 82 and 83 years old, there is no time to waste."

The challenge of change that broke Red's spirit also rewarded him for completing the Change Cycle™. Today he is loved and loving, happy and healthy, and devoted to Myrtle. They are both pushing ninety, still acting like newlyweds, and blessed that life's difficult changes could bring them new love.

We have been so touched by Red's story because it is "our" story. Haven't we all been hurt by the pain of one of the difficult changes that we've experienced? And yet, what a relief that there really is a cycle, an opportunity to come full circle and learn from, grow from, and experience the healing any change can bring. Red experienced every aspect of what we call the Change Cycle™. (Please refer to the color Change Cycle™ in the back of this book.) It gives you a picture of what is happening inside of each and every one of you, young and old, with every change you experience. We encourage you to take the time now to learn about change and welcome the news that, because the stages of change are predictable, each of us can learn to know what to expect of ourselves and others.

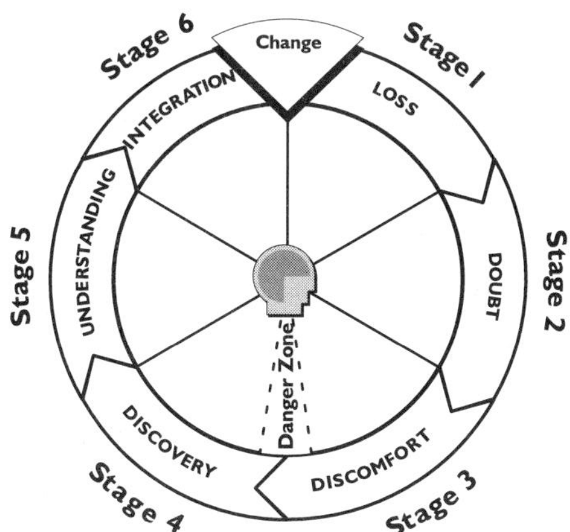

The Change Cycle ™

Although the process or results of change are often viewed as good or bad, change itself is really natural and neutral. On the bright side, change has initiated all of the greatest achievements throughout history. Even before recorded history, change has been the only constant. The very concept of "history," the noting of events happening over time, resulted from the cavepeople's observations of change. The changing of the seasons, the changes in their bodies, the movement of the sun, moon, and stars were dramatic changes that, once acknowledged, were then marked by time. The events of these changes are a simple part of our lives, yet they are powerful reminders that the clock ticks to symbolize that change is ever present. Change has never been an option or a choice on the menu. It is a fact of life—the main fact. A constant. Managing life means managing the changes it brings.

Change is such an integral part of our lives that it becomes our multi-dimensional thermostat. The essence of life comes in our ability to be adaptable. The degree to which we are adaptable is the degree to which we create a healthy emotional, mental, spiritual, and physical state of well-being. When we consider the incredible changes the future will always bring, we understand how critical adapting to the impact of those changes will be on our health and total well-being.

There will continue to be big changes with tremendous social impact. There will also be virtually hundreds of "little" changes that will make our lives faster, safer, easier, healthier.

As society faces the realities of change in the marketplace, the political environment and lifestyles, there will be people who resist change and spend tremendous amounts of time and energy attempting to stop it, or at least delay it. These are common, everyday people; your neighbors, your friends, your family and maybe yourself.

Some find the pace of change so overwhelming, uncomfortable and frightening that fighting for things to stay the same seems a worthy cause. Others want to dictate the behavior and lifestyle choices of others as a way to make everyone "the same" as them.

There are those who feel unable or unwilling to operate in our increasingly technological world and get stuck in yesterday's ways. And, of course there are always those who fight for the status quo even when that means prejudice, injustice, slow progress, and negative long-term consequences.

All of us have been these people to some degree at some time in our lives. Be warned, one of the fuels of prejudice in our world today is the issue of people being unwilling to consider new thoughts, new ideas, new ways. Change always makes something new, or at least different.

For example, because of the continual, gradual increase in the human-life span, individuals of the future are likely to live thirty years longer than people do today. This will create new rules about what it means to retire. Eventually, cancer and heart disease will no longer be life-threatening. There will have to be a new motivation for exercising and eating healthier foods. When these realities set in, so can resistance. These changes all come from external forces and yet, they are a powerful force on our lives and affect the choices and decisions we make.

What about those changes that we initiate on our own? How do we discern our needs, our skills, and our motivation to break the patterns, to give up the sameness? Internal change is a choice. A choice to listen to our inner voice and heed the warnings, the suggestions, the truth. Choice calls us to change and change calls us to break through the fear and the paralysis. We must allow ourselves to change, as well as acknowledge the world changing around us. If we become the hands that fight or resist change, we will miss the personal victories of a better life and the collective benefits of a better world.

Your willingness to both acknowledge and accept that life is now and forever filled with wonderful and painful, profound and simple, easy and aggravating change opportunities. This can be a starting point for your potential to thrive with, instead of succumb to the changes. With an attitude of acceptance and willingness, your inner resources will surface to bring your innate change abilities to light. Like clay to the artist, they mold and shape the present into possibility and then new reality. There is no better choice for successful change than to mix your desire to change with skill.

Desire

We believe that, when you came into the world, God provided an innate sense of desire connected to your heart's purpose. It is that sense of purpose that you must tap into to assist and strengthen you in facing your changes. Desire is an energy that at times pulls, and at times pushes, you toward your goals.

Deep down, each of us carries the desire to become something more than we are; to have the awareness to make the changes. However, there is also within us the fear of giving up what is familiar. If you lose focus, fear becomes what is familiar and adjusting to life means adjusting to fear instead of change. Most of us will admit we are more comfortable if we feel we know what will happen next. And, in a changing situation, a good crystal ball is usually hard to find. Too often, in change situations, we let fear become our measure rather than using desire to be our guide and motivation.

The Paradox

I want to be "better," which is an acknowledgement that I have fallen short of who I believe I am.

Yet, I have allowed fear to keep me in a place where I am less than what I could be.

There is a consequence to this paradox. When we hide in fear from our desire to change, we push our self-esteem lower and lower, and know we are making a choice to be less than our best. This creates a space inside us that is so full of the noise of fear and doubt and anger and prejudice that it literally drowns out our heart's voice of desire to be a better person. When desire goes unanswered, the basis for the motivation to change becomes ineffective. To become a prisoner of fear is to risk that your spirit can be lost in the din of fear's noise. It is essential to silence the fear by facing it, embracing it, letting it go, or leaving it behind, so that desire can once again be discovered.

Because many people are consciously unaware of the sequence of their responses to change, they often choose the "victim" role declaring that these "change things" are happening "to them" and they have no control "over them." This is wrong. We can control our responses to the changes around us. What is happening in our lives is "ours." We must take personal responsibility for it; the good and the bad. Stop and take a look at your life. Is everything just the way you want it? Are you happy and content and willing to stay this way forever? Many of us would honestly say no. We know we are more or want more. That's truth. Let desire motivate you to learn new skills to get there.

There is one thing in any change that is predictable—your personal response to it. As you learn to understand your own responses, you can then effectively share your attitudes and beliefs with others and actually create situations in your life where the changes are understood and even welcomed.

Years ago, Mrs. Miya Einstein was asked by a newspaper reporter, "Do you understand your husband's works such as the Theory of Relativity?" Mrs. Einstein shook her head "no" and replied, "I've never understood any of his theories." She hesitated for just a moment, smiled, and then added, "but I do understand Albert."

The reporter wrote later, "Mrs. Einstein may be the smartest one of all." Maybe it's unnecessary to understand every subtle nuance of change. Maybe it's unnecessary to know why events happen that significantly change our lives. In truth, we can never completely understand the purpose of all the change events that occur in our lives. So to be smartest of all is to learn what your own responses to change are. That awareness will enable you to put desire to work so that you can use change as a catalyst for a better experience of life.

Of course, all the desire in the world will never take the place of skill. They are partners and together skill and desire provide the impetus for successful change.

Throughout history, many cultures, organizations, and individuals have responded to change in much the same way, leaving us valuable information. There is no need to wonder what will happen during the process of change. Because our responses to change are predictable, the ability to deal with change consciously, consistently, and honestly can be easily learned.

Fortunately, there are some people in the world who seem to innately accept and flow with change. This willingness enables them to successfully and easily complete the process of adapting to changing environments and situations. By observing the way they think, their behaviors, attitudes, beliefs, and listening to how they talk to themselves and others about change, it is possible to identify and learn the skills they use to adapt so quickly and so well.

This book is about discovering and strengthening those skills in you. It is now time to step from the unknown and the unsure into a whole new world of change. You can manage your life better when you learn to manage the changes. Choose now to develop or sharpen your skills. When skill and desire meet, your body, mind, and spirit work together to create remarkable results!

What you need is a "road map" for change. A way to know the best route, the detours, the scenic spots, and speed traps. The Change Cycle™ is that map. It will assist you on your journey by providing information for your safety, motivation to move forward, integration for understanding, realization of your beliefs, and the stability to handle, manage, and successfully complete each change process.

"Let us train our minds to desire what the situation demands."

Seneca

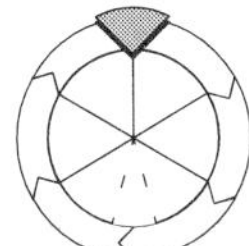

Chapter 2

Change: Rhyme or Reason?

When it comes down to it, change is unavoidable. It's too bad that so many people view it negatively. Unfortunately, most people have grown to accept change as scary, as something over which there is no control. Often people say to us that they feel as if they are being asked to step into the unknown where there are no guarantees. They are right, yet we can improve the odds substantially by understanding how the change process really works. You can unravel the secrets of change by understanding the the six stages of the Change Cycle™.

Interestingly enough, when you look closely at your life, there are many changes that take place every day that would be considered by most as necessary, some important, and all pretty typical.

For example, some of life's everyday simple changes:

- traffic lights
- clothes
- contact lens solution
- shape of the moon

- hair styles
- weather
- time
- TV channels
- the oil in the car
- diapers
- underwear
- kitty litter
- tides
- seasons
- food cravings
- radio stations
- your mind
- the news on TV
- vacuum cleaner bags
- the bibs in the dentist's office

These are simple, everyday changes. Some of them are good, some are inconvenient, some totally mindless and inconsequential. Yet if there was a Gallup Poll on people's basic perception of change, we bet the results would show an overwhelming majority assume that change will create something primarily bad, uncomfortable, and/or painful. This attitude about change is the motivating force behind how our brain stores our change memories and beliefs.

After you have traversed each of the first five stages and reach the final stage in the Change Cycle™, Stage 6, it would certainly be helpful if you would go back into your memories of the change and re-label them more accurately. For instance, "This change started bad, but ended up great!", or "This change was a blessing in disguise." By re-examining your memories of the change, your brain can support you with positive information about the possibilities and potential of change in the future. As a concept, change is broad-based and sometimes difficult, but our responses to it are very predictable. The simple fact is, change is going to happen. The issue then becomes, if change is inevitable and my responses are predictable, then how will I respond?

Predictable Responses To Change

There are four predictable responses to change and they provide the basic foundation for understanding your thoughts, feelings, and behaviors when faced with any change. Your brain consistently follows the same path and plan each time. By noticing your responses and reactions, you will be able to recognize and eventually alter, strengthen, or create new change responses. Though our individual experiences add uniqueness to each change process, the basic path remains the same for all of us.

There are four predictable responses of the brain to change:

- The brain distorts, deletes, and generalizes new information.
- The brain makes no differentiations between "good" or "bad" changes.
- The brain makes no differentiation between externally imposed or internally driven changes.
- The brain responds multi-dimensionally.

Let's look at each one of these responses a little more closely.

The Brain Distorts, Deletes, and Generalizes New Information

In 1977, a study of the brain's sorting and associating patterns was conducted by psychologists R.C. Schank and R.P. Abelson. Their subjects were shown a typical business office. They were allowed to look for two minutes and they were then asked to list everything they saw in the office. When the researchers studied the lists of each participant, they found three consistent results:

1. The items on the participant's list that were accurate were things that are typically found in an office (for example, desk, typewriter, pens, pencils, clock).
2. Participants listed things that were not in the picture but are normally in an office (for example, chair, books, telephone).
3. Participants failed to list things that were in the picture but are not normally in an office (for example, toaster and picnic basket).

Early researchers named this phenomenon of superimposing historic information onto a current event *schema*, which means to form a pattern based on past experience for use at present and in the future. As the brain takes in new stimuli, if there is no current information in the long-term memory, your brain provides, through schema, an association to the closest memory of related information.

The operation of schema in perception causes the initial picture of a change situation to be inaccurate. Every time something new comes in, the brain deletes, distorts, or

The Fine Art of Schema

generalizes the information since it can only use similar situations to create a picture of the new experience. For example:

> **Deleted:** Some pieces of the change situation are missed entirely.
>
> **Generalized:** Some pieces of the change situation are perceived accurately, because they match part of a past experience and can be transferred to the new experience.
>
> **Distorted:** Some pieces are added to the change situation that don't really exist. Generally, they are a combination of past experiences.

Schema is a very important concept and resource. It can provide clarity and direction. Be warned though, it has an equal chance of creating confusion and chaos because the mental picture is historical, not current, and almost always, in part, inaccurate.

The brain's system of coding information is straightforward: observe change, label or evaluate it (good or bad is as complex as it usually gets), and store it. The following example should give you an idea.

After having a blood test, the doctor reports to Sandy that her cholesterol is higher than credit card interest rates and an immediate change in dietary habits is necessary. The change is presented as the "healthy solution," but the prospect of giving up cheeseburgers sounds more like a call to an exclusion of all foods that taste good.

Sandy's brain is busy taking in the doctor's orders and warnings and immediately stores this change by her initial conscious and unconscious mental, emotional, and behavioral responses:

Emotional: "No cheeseburgers? I feel cheated already!"

Mental: "I think this is impossible with my schedule."

Behavioral: "I'll do what I can, but..."

The brain has set up the system to handle only "good" and "bad" changes, but no consistent criteria for how, why, or when to make the determinations. Having learned by experience, Sandy's brain knows she has a pattern of reacting to change by feeling bad, uncomfortable, inconvenienced, fearful, resistant, and "picked on." Sandy's brain determines that the message was very clear; Sandy is unhappy, no need to investigate further, and stamps a big red "bad change" label on the experience and stores the memory accordingly. Most people have an overwhelming number of "bad change" files. This is sad, since the truth about any change (good or bad) is that it is rarely accurately described because the brain labels and stores it too early in the process, generally relying on initial emotional responses as the main criteria.

The Brain Makes No Differentiations Between "Good" or "Bad" Changes

When a new change stimulus enters your brain, it triggers the process that produces your mental, emotional, and/or physical responses. This response, or in some cases reaction, is consistently the same regardless of the nature of the change. For example, winning the lottery could be considered a "good" change, while losing your health insurance might be considered a "bad" change. However, in your brain, the experiences of these changes produces the same sequential response at the unconscious level. Although it may seem that the perception of good versus bad would change the sequence or nature of our responses, it doesn't, because of the brain will process new information the same way regardless of the label we put on it. Consequently, the change response is affected by the good or bad perception only in the areas of time and intensity. (This relationship will be addressed later.) This is an important concept to understand as you learn your response to change patterns.

The Brain Makes No Differentiation Between Externally Imposed or Internally Driven Changes

It would be a reasonable conclusion to assume that when you decide to make a change (internally driven), your response would be different than if you have a change imposed on you (externally driven). However, your brain has no filter for internal versus external cause and treats the change in its standard manner.

For example, if you choose to go on a diet to lose weight, it is a change that you have decided to make; an internally driven change. If your home is heavily damaged by a storm, this is a change that has been imposed on you from another or external source. In both cases, your responses to the change will be the same.

Admittedly, it is easy to think that something you decide or choose to change might create a more positive response. The key is to remember that, by the time you "act" on your decision to change, you will have already gone through your initial set of negative responses, perhaps unaware of some of those responses. With externally imposed change, it is easier to be aware of direct correlations between the onset of the change and your initial set of responses.

The Brain Responds Multi-Dimensionally

With any kind of stimuli, the brain will respond on many levels. We all have emotional, behavioral, spiritual, and mental filters that produce simultaneous responses in varying degrees. So, it is important to look for clues in all these areas. As humans, we are not be one-dimensional creatures. If we were, we would act only out of instinct, as most other animal species do; without thought or emotion.

Unpredictable Responses To Change

Time of Response

Each person takes varying degrees of time to work through all the issues that surround change. For example, a single, childless woman who finds out she is unexpectedly pregnant (and with twins) will probably take longer to go through all of the stages of change than a married mother of two who has found out that she is pregnant with a child for which she has carefully planned.

In other words, the time element is an individual variable and, without detailed knowledge of an individual's psychological profile and sorting patterns in the brain, time cannot be predicted.

Intensity of Response

As we allow our brains to process new changes, we will find that individual filters produce different levels of intensity about that change. Intensity can also be affected by the nature of the change. For example, a filing system change at work will certainly be less intense than losing health insurance benefits. When we add the individual filters to the circumstance of the change, we find a variable that is difficult to predict.

The relationship between time and intensity is that intensity motivates time. This works in two different ways. Some people are motivated to move quickly to adapt to change because the intensity is so profound. Other people go through change much more slowly because the experience is so intense, they have difficulty adapting.

The Need For A Map

Often, people facing change resemble a couple packing their car for a vacation to a specific destination, yet with no idea about how to get there and no map to assist them.

You can imagine what must be happening in the brain in order to prepare for the trip. Since there is no route, no plan, no map, then the logical conclusion of the brain is to look through its memories for past vacations and by using association skills and schema, to retrieve historical information. This can be very cumbersome. If you have been on a camping trip in the mountains and a vacation on the beach, then your brain pulls up all "vacation" information and you will find yourself putting everything from suntan lotion and a beach ball to a down jacket and wool socks in your suitcase.

Our journey through change often resembles this. We begin it with no map, very few skills, and a file clerk in our brain who is retrieving our historical change experiences. If that history happens to be saved as negative (and often is), then we're also predisposed to perceiving the journey as not being any fun or bad.

Now that you have learned how your filing system works, you need a good, clean, accurate, and easy-to-use *change map*. The Change Cycle™ is that map. It exists within you, and now is the time to learn how it will help you determine where you are and in what direction to move, anticipate possible problems or slow-downs, and measure the distance from where you are to where you want to be. Basically, it enables you to plot the quickest, easiest, lowest risk way to get through any change.

The Change Cycle™ map, shown on the following page, is depicted as a circle to show the continuous and cyclical nature of change in our lives. The first humans noticed cycles in the days and nights, the weather and their own bodies. These observations led to the need for and the development of time to mark the seasons and cycles. Clearly, everything in nature is process-driven and therefore cyclical. The migration south of some birds during the winter months or the hibernation of bears, follows cycles that are predictable and are designed to assist them in responding to the changing seasons. Because we are a part of the same forces of nature that created other animals, we too operate on cycles in some parts of our lives.

The Change Cycle™

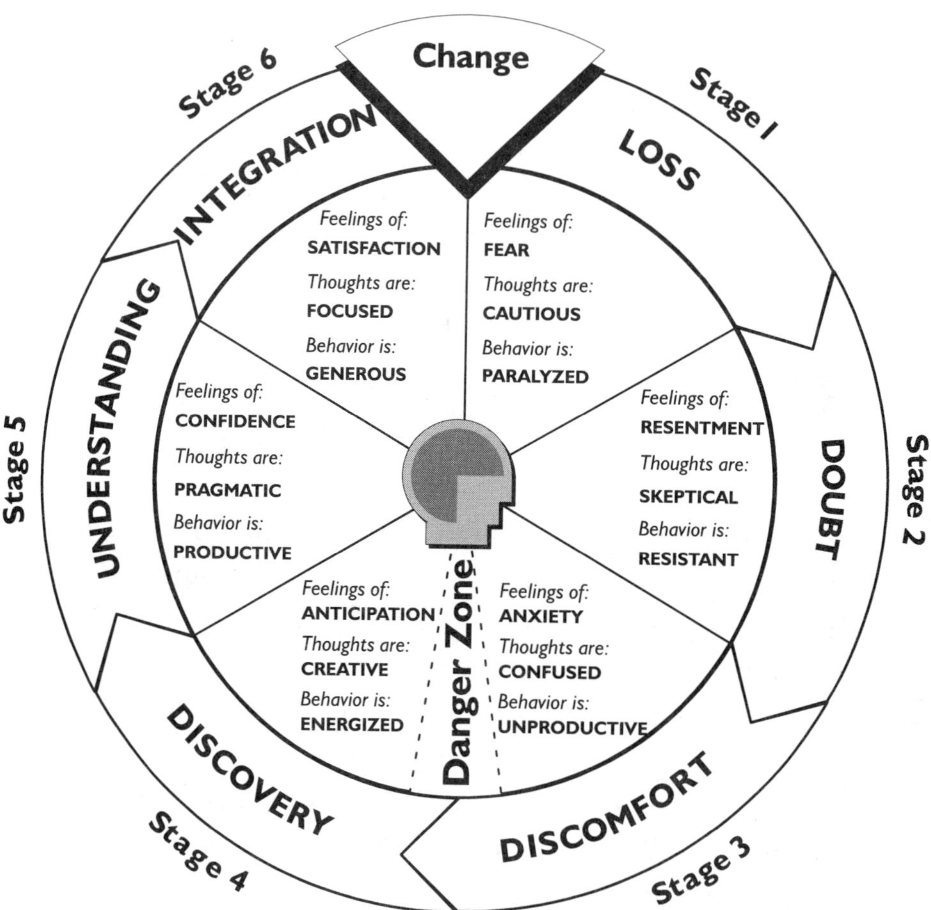

When a change enters your life, (shown as the blue triangle at the top center), the Change Cycle™ begins. Because all change affects you at the emotional, behavioral, and mental levels, understanding your feelings, behaviors, and thoughts becomes the vital tool in assisting you to take personal responsibility for the changes you face. In the center, there is an image of the brain, because the unconscious mind works in a sequential way (with or without the conscious mind's awareness), to sort out the new experience.

The Change Cycle™ model represents the series of six "Stages" you will pass through in dealing with any change. The outside ring, Loss, Doubt, Discomfort, Discovery, Understanding, and Integration, indicates what the primary experience is for that Stage. Each of the six Stages is shaped like a pie piece and the colors, red, yellow, and green, are used to symbolically indicate a traffic light. The first two Stages and The Danger Zone are the color red to warn you to stop and be observant of potential danger coming from other directions. Stages 3 and 4 are yellow to signal the need for some amount of caution. Your responses in the yellow Stage will probably be similar to what you do when faced with a yellow light while driving. Do you immediately slow down to stop, knowing that the red light is next, or do you hit the gas and get through the intersection quickly? Stages 5 and 6 are green to indicate freedom of forward movement. In each Stage, the primary feeling, behavior, and mental aspects of your response to change are listed. Remember, each characteristic is representative of a wide range of possible thoughts, feelings, or behaviors and, of course, all three are happening simultaneously.

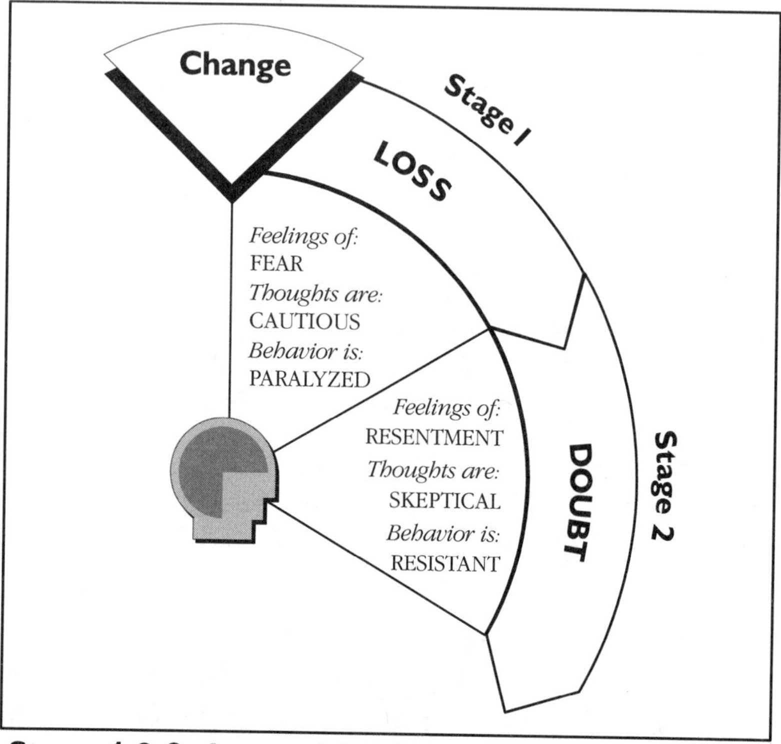

Stages 1 & 2—Loss and Doubt

During the red Stages, 1, Loss and 2, Doubt, your thoughts, feelings, and behaviors are consistently converse or opposite to what you need to accomplish in order to move forward. Moving through your fears to find safety is the foundation for the successful completion of any change.

Stage 3, Discomfort, and Stage 4, Discovery, are yellow to symbolize the need for caution. During Stage 3, forward motion is critical in order to create the momentum to "turn the corner" through The Danger Zone and move toward the green Stages. Stages 3 and 4 are the beginning of your shift to assimilating new information and working with it to formulate viable options.

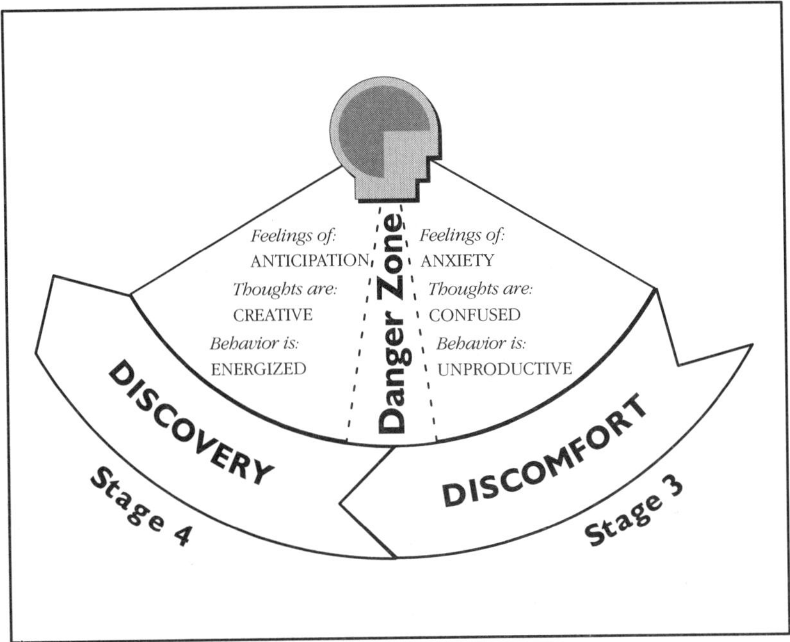

Stages 3 & 4– Discomfort and Discovery

Looming at the bottom of the Change Cycle™, and between Stages 3 and 4, is The Danger Zone. Beware, The Danger Zone is where your inability or unwillingness to continue forward progress (because of confusion, lethargic behavior, or anxiety) recreates fear and a lack of safety, thus looping you back to Stage 1. This typical pattern of looping back to Stage 1 is one of the reasons your long-term memory has encoded negative experiences with change. This coding can be updated by adding successfully completed change experiences.

The final Stages, 5, Understanding, and 6, Integration, are green. At this point, the original change has become such a part of the individual that it is unlikely to be labeled as a change at all.

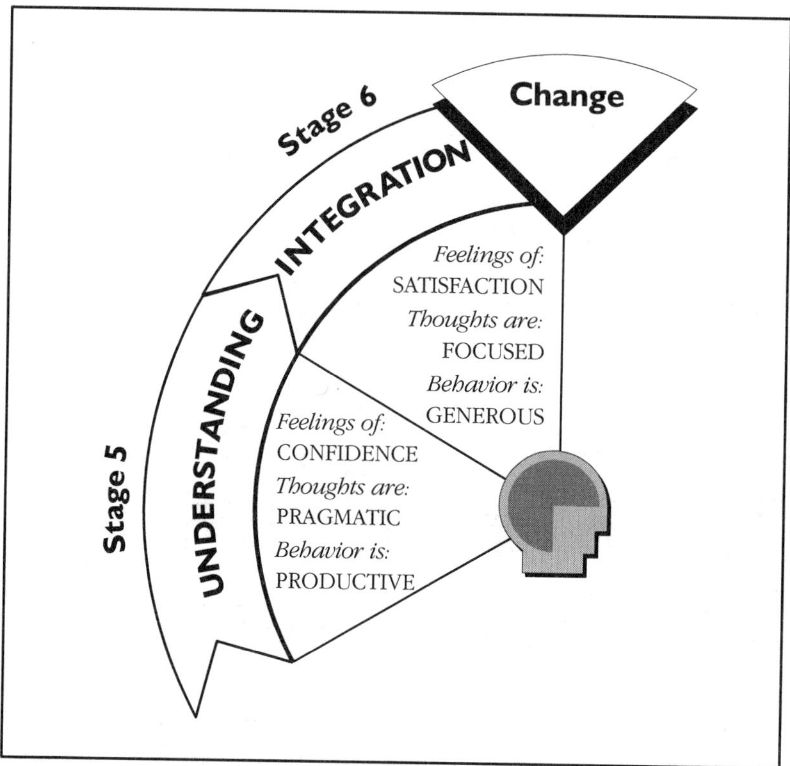

Stages 5 & 6—Understanding and Integration

By using the Change Cycle™ as your navigation map, you will be able to identify your needs and utilize your skills to complete your change processes in a healthier and more positive way.

No map will do you any good if you don't know where you are to begin. The Change Cycle Locator™, a simple yet profound self-assessment tool for you to use to pinpoint the specific issues you are experiencing within a change.

By assessing the thoughts, feelings and behaviors that characterize your current attitudes toward a specific change process, it focuses in on where you are in the Change Cycle™. This knowledge enables you to ask the right questions, select the right strategies and take the right action to move toward successful completion of your change situation.

If you have one, please take the time now to complete the Change Cycle Locator™ so you can use your results to measure how you will improve your change skills as you learn about and move through the Change Cycle™.

Pinpointing the Change

The key to obtaining accurate results is in defining or pinpointing the specific change. Because any change is multi-faceted and therefore, can be over generalized, staying focused on one clear aspect of the change will give you the best results.

A. Name the change.

B. What specific losses does **A** create for me?

C. Which one in **B** is most important to me now?

D. Why?

Using your previous answers, fill in the following:

Even though **A** is a big change, the immediate issue for me is the loss in (**C**)____________________________
because of (**D**) ____________________________.

Your answers to **C** and **D** indicate the actual aspect of the change that is driving your thoughts, feelings, and behavior. Focus on it as you learn more about each stage of the Change Cycle™.

"Small things done in strategic places create major impact."

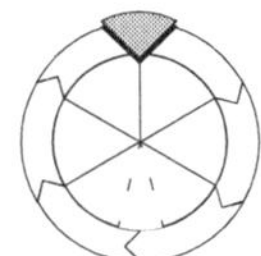

Chapter 3

Change: Who Does It Best?

Fortunately, there are some people on the planet who actually enjoy change, seek it out, work with it, and successfully use it to get what they desire. They thrive on change. Though relatively small in number, there are some people who seem to have the innate ability to adapt quickly and easily in change situations. These individuals are the ones for us to look to as models.

We call these people *Successful Changers*. Our research and study is based on their consistent patterns of thought, feelings, and behaviors in changing situations and environments. We will refer to them often and hope they provide you with new insight into how you can learn to become a *Successful Changer* too. As you observe *Successful Changers*, notice there are some definite distinctions in their attitudes, beliefs, behaviors, and results. To further develop your skills in successfully completing any change process, these distinctions become very useful. *Successful Changers* are the people who provide us with the information needed to navigate through the sometimes stormy waters of change.

It is important to notice the dimensions of a *Successful Changer's* internal processing of information and their behavior. It all comes down to the attitudes and beliefs they live by and the skills they use. The encouraging news from studying *Successful Changers* is this: If you practice the skills that they use, over time you can develop the same attitudes and beliefs that motivate them.

We can model, and therefore, recreate for ourselves their success. By integrating basic, positive attitudes and beliefs about change and combining them with the right skills (or tools), any of us can learn to adapt and flourish in changing environments and situations. Is it easy? Not always. Is it simple? Yes. *Successful Changers* do it almost unconsciously. For them, it is a habit, a way of life. Can we do that? Of course. Like any new activity or function, it takes awhile to get used to it, but over time, we learn and integrate, and then do it without thinking. Won't it be great to get to the point where you can cruise through change situations because you know how you feel, what you want, what to expect from yourself, and what actions to take? By becoming a *Successful Changer* you know how to manage your life by managing the changes.

Successful Changer Attitudes And Beliefs

Attitudes and beliefs play into the change equation as internal processes that affect external actions. These two characteristics alone give big clues as to what is driving a person's behavior. It is helpful to think of attitudes and beliefs as internal binoculars that contribute significantly to the way a person sees the world. Since everyone's perspective is a little different, it is interesting to notice the similarities of beliefs and attitudes in *Successful Changers* to understand how they develop their views. We refer to attitudes here to describe a person's primary perspective; the way one looks at things and then how one decides what to do. Attitudes determine how we see ourselves, as well as other people, and we integrate that knowledge into our life experiences. Beliefs are the basic truths which form the foundation from which we take action. Our belief systems are set up to assist us in being consistent and true to ourselves and our value systems. *Successful Changers* commonly share basic attitudes and beliefs.

In his profound book, *Illusions*, Richard Bach stated, "Argue for your limitations and sure enough, they're yours." Most of us have been guilty at least once for expecting the worst and thus, only focusing on the problem. *Successful Changers* consistently use their positive attitudes and beliefs to expend their energy on acting out their belief that there are no limits to solving their problems or change situations. In order for you to develop these beliefs and attitudes, there must be a commitment to thinking in a new way. Of course, this takes practice.

5 Basic Attitudes Of Successful Changers

1. I am eager to learn something in every situation.
2. I am grateful for what I have and where I am.
3. I have a clear picture of how I want this change to turn out.
4. It is important to me to continually take action toward my positive outcome.
5. I have something to learn from and offer this experience.

4 Fundamental Beliefs Of Successful Changers

1. I believe that change is a normal and necessary part of life.
2. I believe that I must take responsibility for what has happened, what is happening, and how I feel.
3. I believe that change can be an adventure and a challenge that ultimately brings out the best in me.
4. I believe that I can handle whatever happens in my life.

Skills For Managing Change

Utilize Internal Resources

Ask any driver, young or old, to reel off a list of safe driving tips and they'll probably come up with some of these: never drink and drive, always fasten your seatbelt, and stay within the speed limit.

When life gets complicated and busy, safety often takes a back seat. Getting to your dentist appointment on time becomes more important than honoring the speed limit. Keeping your clothes from getting wrinkled becomes more important than wearing a seatbelt. Drinking, impressing friends, and then getting behind the wheel becomes more important than allowing someone else to drive you home. Many of us have been guilty of at least one of these at one time or another and some of us have even suffered severe consequences because of these choices. Sometimes we are easily steered away from the basic resources we typically know or use by the multiple distractions that enter our chaotic world on any given day.

This basic scenario also plays itself out when you face the change process. Fortunately, you have plenty of internal resources to make the journey easier and safer. Unfortunately, in the midst of sometimes overwhelming distractions created by the change, it is easy to leave those internal resources untapped.

Internal resources are the qualities within us that can be utilized as tools. We all have different tools available depending on the job that's needed. For example, a good hammer is the best tool to connect a nail with a piece of wood, but we all know that in the absence of a hammer, a large rock or sturdy shoe will get the job done!

One of the best examples of using internal resources in nature is the behavior of the lion family. These beautiful animals use their internal resources of loyalty, courage, and responsibility to maintain their "pride" or family unit. Each adult lion has the responsibility to protect their family, and they do. The internal resources that lions draw on consistently make them the kings and queens of the jungle. The term, "survival of the fittest," is generally used to refer to the animal kingdom because it is their innate ability to adapt to changing environments and stay alive generation after generation. The ability to adapt is in large part due to their gut instinct to call forth, on a timely basis, that which is strong and useful within themselves—their internal resources.

When modeling someone else's behavior, notice what they value, depend on, and give attention to. This essentially adds up to be a list of their strongest internal resources.

Successful Changers frequently use these nine basic internal resources first, and then augment them with others:

- Commitment
- Creativity
- Focus
- Responsibility
- Truthfulness
- Discipline
- Courage
- Humor
- Perspective

Just as good drivers keep safe driving principles constantly in mind, *Successful Changers* are aware of these internal resources all the time.

Perhaps some of your internal resources have become rusty with lack of use. This only means that you need to use these tools more often to get them back in shape. The more resources we have available, the better our chances for success.

Some examples of your available internal resources:

- Creativity
- Spontaneity
- Love
- Humor
- Tenacity
- Desire
- Perspective
- Faith
- Perseverance
- Integrity
- Focus
- Trust
- Commitment
- Loyalty
- Courage
- Discipline
- Compassion
- Responsibility

Underneath the masks or facades we all have designed to deal with the world, at least some of these resources are inside us. Using them is what keeps us alive and healthy. In fact, many people with serious mental illnesses falsely think they are void of these resources, or deny them.

Suffice it to say, we all have access to the incredible strength internal resources provide us. They are ours to use as we want or need. Remember, if you have ever once tapped into one of these internal resources, then you have proven to yourself that it truly does exist within you!

Use Supportive Language

One of the most dramatic differences between *Successful Changers* and others is their use of language. It seems that *Successful Changers* somehow understand that what they say to themselves and to others has an impact on their behavior. Every word that is said (out loud, as well as self-talk) is internalized by the unconscious mind. These words are the catalyst for your behaviors, thoughts, and emotions. The truth is that we talk to ourselves just like we talk to others. We need to be careful to choose our words wisely. *Successful Changers* are outstanding models of how useful our language can be.

A study with professional athletes on self-talk provided some very interesting results. The entire group was asked what they felt going into big games. Some of the athletes clearly described and labeled the feeling "anticipation" and the others claimed they were nervous and felt varying degrees of "anxiety." All of these athletes were highly skilled, highly trained, and highly paid, yet their self-talk had significant impact on how they performed. Those who named the feeling "anxiety" tended to make little mistakes. Those who named it "anticipation" tended to be the ones who made the incredible plays. Interestingly enough, physiologically we have identical responses to anxiety and anticipation. In other words, our heart rate, breathing, adrenaline flow, brain wave patterns, and muscle tension are exactly the same when experiencing either of these two emotions.

It appears that the difference in performance had to do with what the athletes named the feeling and the self-talk that followed. This points to the importance of language. How we name our thoughts and feelings and express them becomes critical. *Successful Changers* are masters at using language that supports them in feeling better, motivating them to get what they want and to do what needs to be done.

The language patterns most often used by Successful Changers are:

"Even if ___ feels bad, the good thing about it is ___."

"There are people and past experiences that can help me go through this better."

"I always have options."

"What I want to get out of this is ______."

"It is my responsibility to grow and learn through this."

"I have some ideas about how to make this easier."

"This is exciting—an adventure!"

A *Successful Changer* will admit that sometimes they say these things to themselves because they need to be convinced. They also admit that sometimes they have doubts even when they use these language patterns. However, when these "positive words" are going into our minds and the minds of others, it helps to encourage possibilities, different options, and actions. *Successful Changers* are quick to note that when they allow themselves to get involved in negative verbal expressions, they can quickly end up in a downward spiral. They also know they must immediately break the pattern by switching to positive, resourceful words.

Isn't it obvious that our words have a powerful effect on us? Listen to what you say to yourself and then change some of your old vocabulary habits by speaking powerful, positive words and thoughts. Your words are supporting you for something. Make sure it is for something you really want. Again, it will take practice. Eventually it will become a natural habit. This new vocabulary will contribute to your motivation to make change an easy part of life. Talking to yourself can be very productive!

Your Position In The Change Process

Successful Changers also have a knack for pinpointing specifically where they are in the Change Cycle™. They also develop a relationship with the change right away rather than attempting to keep it separate from them. This is one of the major keys to expediting the process of adapting and minimizing the potential for conflict.

Picture yourself as the captain of a yacht on the ocean. Suddenly a bad storm begins to move in. To outrun the storm is unlikely and dangerous. On the other hand, if you immediately begin to identify where you are in relationship to the storm, you'll find many more options emerge. For example, you may see that with a slight move eastward, you will almost certainly be on the outside of the storm and will be affected minimally. Or, it may become obvious that there is no threat of lightning so covering up and sitting through the rain might be the best option. Maybe calling the Coast Guard on the radio for a weather update will show that because of the swift wind, the storm is going to blow over quickly, but you will need to prepare for a short time of rough water.

The point is to navigate through change by pinpointing your location and considering the options that present themselves. When you operate from a reactionary state and fail to check your position, you set yourself up to have very few options. Navigating through change is about options, choices, and riding the waves.

The rest of this book is dedicated to translating the beliefs, attitudes, and skills of *Successful Changers* in such a way that you can use them in your life.

When you have finished, you will be different. Your mind will have expanded to take in new ideas and skills and your very being will probably breathe a sigh of relief because you know now that change is in your control.

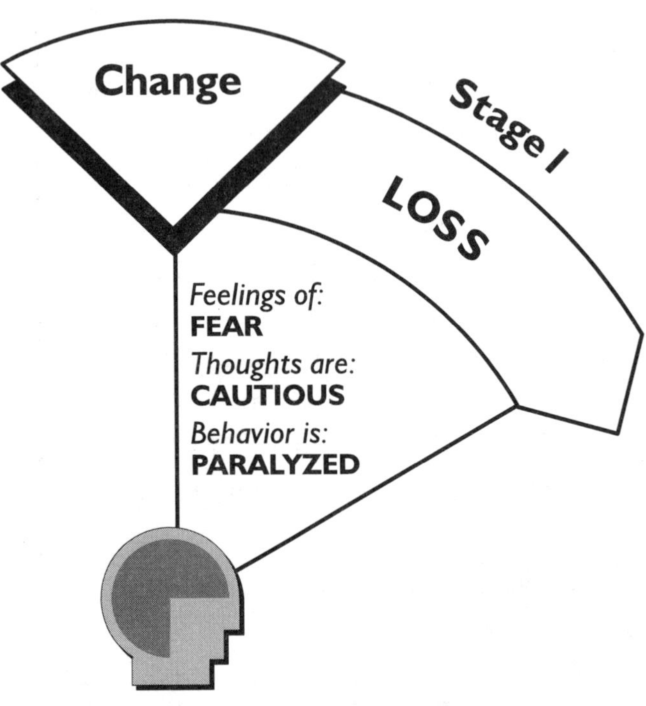

Stage 1—The Change Against Me	
Primary Experience:	Loss
Major Focus:	Self-protection
Stage Objective:	Creating personal safety
Motivated By:	Pain or security
Overuses:	Paranoia
Challenge:	Defeating the "endless victim" mentality
Opportunity:	Learning to channel fear into appropriate action

"In a fight between you and the world,
bet on the world."

Franz Kafka

Chapter 4

The Change Against Me

Stage 1: Loss

In the cartoon above, the triangle is our symbol for change. We have named this character "Charlie". He/she models a changing personality at the start of each Stage chapter.

Quite literally, in Stage 1 you feel as though the change is out to get you. When this happens, you experience a sense of losing control and you may see yourself as "the victim." Stage 1 is also the point at which you first become aware that you are experiencing both the arrival of something new and the loss of something familiar. It is important to remember this because you often expect yourself or others to immediately accept something new, when in reality the first issue is to deal with the loss of what has been. It is a fact that no two "objects" can occupy the same space. If something "new" is coming into our experience, something else must be removed or moved aside. The primary struggle in Stage 1 is dealing with the losses that will be experienced as a result of the change we're facing.

A common misperception is that when we talk about loss, we're only talking about it in relationship to changes that are "bad." But, if you think for a minute, you'll probably be able to remember changes in your life that you considered "good," yet there was still the experience of loss. For example: a new car, your first child, high school graduation, a promotion, marriage.

What might the losses have been in these experiences? Marriage might mean the loss of independence, disposable income, free time, etc. A promotion at work might bring the loss of co-workers, a loss of confidence in your job area, or the loss of friends and home because a move is required. A friend of ours bought a used car a few months ago in order to reduce her monthly expenses. She previously had a luxury car and needed to down-scale to save money. Her new car was really nice, but for a while she really suffered with the loss of space, status, and all the bells and whistles. No matter what the change, there is some kind of loss to deal with.

As you learn about Stage 1, acknowledge that loss is a natural part of change. It is neither good nor bad. What we do with our attitude can create a perspective that can vary the results. The negative pole would slide you into paralysis and powerlessness. The positive pole would create a sense of safety. Allow the rest of this Chapter to assist you in learning how to produce a positive result when you find yourself in Stage 1.

What Does Stage 1 Look Like?

At age twenty-one, Thad was the captain of his college tennis team, an honor student, and looking ahead to law school. Without warning, that all came to an abrupt halt. Although he had been feeling bad physically, Thad thought it was just the pressures of school. Eventually there came a point when Thad could barely function and he finally went to the doctor. Thad was suffering with hepatitis and the other miserable effects caused by an overactive thyroid. After several misdiagnoses and with his body weakening, Thad found out he had developed Graves Disease.

The doctors informed Thad that the only treatment was to ingest a container of radioactive iodine, which would essentially eliminate his thyroid gland. Feeling left with no choice, Thad agreed to the procedure. When he was taken to the treatment room, the impact of all that was happening really hit him. His body was creating changes that he never imagined. A heavy metal vest was placed over his chest and extended down onto his legs. The technician entered the room wearing a virtual suit of armor, including a mask that resembled one worn by a welder. Suddenly, Thad experienced incredible fear. "What if this doesn't work? What if my only option goes wrong? How can my body hold up under any more punishment?" For a moment, he wanted to "freeze" everything. He felt paralyzed by his lack of options. In that moment, the fear was overwhelming and nothing seemed safe. He wondered why the doctors seemed so unconcerned about the outcome when he wanted them to be cautious and very caring. Thad knew he had to trust the doctors, but he also knew that Graves Disease could lead to death.

As you begin to understand Stage 1 of the Change Cycle™, remember Thad. Notice that his story articulates the issues that emerge in Stage 1. As he faced the radioactive iodine, Thad essentially faced the ultimate loss—his life. Because, if the dye didn't work, there seemed to be no other alternatives. Being faced with that kind of loss caused Thad to have some understandable feelings of fear, thoughts that were cautious and uncertain, and signs of paralyzed behavior.

Although few of us stare death in the face as Thad did, we do experience this kind of fear in the face of overwhelming change. Sometimes it is only for a moment and sometimes it is sustained over a longer period of time. Either way, it is a very real experience and one very much associated with the initial awareness of change. Thad had to deal with the potential and real loss this change would create before he could embrace what was left and what could be gained.

As Thad now reflects on that day, he realizes that everyone (especially his doctors) saw the treatment as a safe and sure bet, an option that would absolutely work. The only fear existed inside Thad. In retrospect, he knows that his fear was unfounded, yet it was painfully real at the time. And, he also knows that his fear came because of what he had to lose. Today, Thad is healthy, happily married, and a successful attorney. Of course, he still remembers the fear surrounding those tentative days before his successful treatment created the safety to move forward through the change experience by regaining his health.

With this story as a backdrop, let's take a closer look at the feelings, thoughts, and behaviors in Stage 1.

Feelings of Fear

The primary emotion in Stage 1 is fear. With change comes loss; with loss comes fear. There is fear of what life will be like without that person, process, possession, or habit. There is fear about how you will be affected by the "new" change. There is fear that someone or something else is in control of you and your life. There is fear of the known and of the unknown. These fears are expressed as hurt, frustration, defensiveness, and even paranoia.

FEAR

Fear is an emotion that has both an up and a down side. On the up side, fear keeps you alert and can warn you in dangerous situations. On the down side, fear can paralyze you and keep you from taking appropriate action. Fear is a natural part of Stage 1 and you can learn to use it to create safety.

If most of us unexpectedly happen upon a big snake in the woods, we experience fear. At that moment, the most important thing to do is get to a place of safety; as far away from the snake as you can get. The intention of fear is to protect us and urge us to move away from danger. Fear only becomes a negative when we hold on to it or fail to be motivated by it to find safety. Once we're safe from the danger, it is okay to let the fear go and begin to consider how we might avoid that danger in the future.

The problem comes when we hold onto the fear far beyond its original purpose of protection. In the case of the snake, it might mean some would choose to never go into the woods again. What a loss. Fear is a warning that we feel inadequate to handle or cope with a situation. That understanding is the first step to relieving the fear. When you are in Stage 1, notice any tendency you might have to hold onto fear because it will cause you to "make up" other fears that don't really exist. This will only keep you stuck in Stage 1.

We can never underestimate the power of our negative imagination. Like Thad, many people recount that when the change is over, they realize that most of their fears in the beginning were unwarranted and never came true.

Of course, that doesn't keep fear away, but it does give us insight into the trials we put ourselves through when fear comes on the scene. Though fear is a real emotion, most of the time it is created from an imagined negative expectation.

Thoughts Are Cautious

When you are experiencing fear and paralysis, it is little wonder that your brain sends signals that you need to be cautious. On the up side, when cautious thoughts operate to help you, they assist you with thinking before you take action and support you in watching for the traps and loopholes in your decision making. If nothing else, this caution helps you to formulate questions that need and deserve answers.

However, the down side is that if cautious thinking prevails for too long, it will eventually turn into paranoia. And, of course, paranoid thinking only fuels the fire of fear and aggravates paralysis. Hanging on to caution can often be the hidden culprit of being stuck in a rut, because it can be disguised for awhile as a reasonable and rational response to the chaos going on around you.

Obviously, when you are experiencing fear and paralysis, the world feels very unsafe. According to Abraham Maslow, creating emotional and physical safety are our greatest needs after basic survival (food, water, sleep). When safety is threatened, our fundamental well-being is significantly altered. To move to Stage 2, your efforts need to be centered around creating safety for yourself. So, in Stage 1, it is imperative that you learn to recognize where you are, practice what *Successful Changers* do, and establish a sense of safety.

Behavior Is Paralyzed

The primary behavior in Stage 1 is paralysis; becoming trapped or unable to move forward because of fear. When we experience fear, our innate response is to do one of these:

- Flee by running away and denying the change.
- Freeze or become paralyzed and stay firmly rooted in Stage 1.
- Fight as a way of defending yourself against the change, which creates or embraces conflict instead of providing safety.

On the one side, paralysis can be useful as a way of stopping to take stock of the situation. Temporary paralysis may assist you in identifying your losses and facing them honestly. It may also help you to assess exactly where you are and what you need to do to create some safety in the midst of unsettling situations.

On the other side, when you are paralyzed for an extended amount of time, eventually you can become too dependent on other people to take care of you, have trouble doing simple tasks, and fail to take care of your basic needs. This is a result of giving up your personal power and feeling victimized.

Look at the behaviors and language patterns produced by feelings of Loss in the table below.

People Who Are Struggling With Loss	
Behaviors	
• Feelings of powerlessness • Imagining the same old results • Putting up walls • Generalizing negative behaviors and emotions into other areas of life	
Language Patterns	
• "I don't know who to trust." • "What have I done to deserve this?" • "This won't really change anything." • "I'm going to just keep my feelings to myself."	
Word Descriptions	
• Threatened • Helpless • Distrusting • Inward Oppression • Destined for Doom	• Denial • Victimized • Frozen • Self-pity

What Do Successful Changers Do?

The Jim MacLaren Story

Eight years ago, Jim MacLaren was pronounced dead-on-arrival at Bellevue Hospital in New York after his motorcycle was broadsided by a 40,000-pound metro bus in mid-town Manhattan. After being revived and spending six days in a coma, Jim awoke to find that his left leg had been amputated below the knee. The doctors informed him that his rehabilitation would take many, many months, but he astounded the medical community when he left the hospital after only eleven days and returned to acting school at Yale University in less than three months. Jim began swimming, bicycling, and running with a prosthetic leg, and went on to set world records in marathons, triathlons, and even the Ironman Triathlon in Hawaii. He became a sought after motivational speaker and even did a stint on the daytime drama, *Another World*. Jim spoke of living through the changes, making positive choices, and how he is turning his disability into a gift.

Little did Jim know as he left his home in Boulder, Colorado, on June 5, 1993, to compete in a triathlon in Southern California and film a feature segment for CNN, that his life would take another dramatic turn and that his ability to respond to tremendous change would once again be put to a rigorous test. While competing, Jim's bicycle was struck by a van which had illegally entered the bike course of the triathlon. He was thrown headfirst into a lightpost, breaking the fifth and sixth cervical vertebrae in his neck. Jim was diagnosed as a quadriplegic and was given little hope for regaining sensation and movement in his arms and legs. He remained in intensive care in California for over three weeks, enduring three surgeries on his neck, and was then transferred to Craig Rehabilitation Hospital in Denver, one of the finest spinal rehabilitation hospitals in the world. The long and arduous task of recovery and rehabilitation began slowly and painfully. He began to recover some sensation in his body and even began moving his arms.

It became evident that anyone who said he'd never recover, didn't know Jim. Miraculously, he began moving his legs and, under the careful supervision of his therapists, Jim MacLaren took his first steps on October 4th. Although he is a long way from walking functionally and still needs continuous care, Jim is walking further each day, lifting weights, working in the pool, and quietly preparing to set up a new lifestyle. Jim plans to continue speaking, teaching and sharing the knowledge he's gained since his accidents—that each person has a "disability." In other words, a challenge that he or she must deal with in life.

"Everyone takes a leg off at night, in a sense," says MacLaren. "Maybe your challenge is getting along with your father. Everything is relative. I believe that there are no limits on any of us and that we all have the power to take control of our lives. Life is a gift and a challenge for each of us," Jim says. "The trick is not to label our change experiences as 'good' or 'bad,' but to accept them as a part of life, so that we can learn the lessons we must learn to realize our full potential. We're here on earth for a reason and after my injury, I was faced with finding out what mine was. If someone offered me my leg back, I wouldn't want it. I am a different and better person because of the accident. This trauma and my loss has been a gift in a lot of ways."

Jim's story is typical of other *Successful Changers* because we can identify three primary skills he uses to achieve a sense of safety. As you read through these skills note how easy they can be for you to incorporate into your new change habits.

The following table shows the behavior and language patterns *Successful Changers* use to help themselves manage fear and create a feeling of safety.

People Who Are Successful Creating Safety	
Behaviors	
• Having a clear definition of the change. • Creating clear outcomes. • Knowing the real fears versus the imagined fears.	
Language Patterns	
• "This is scary, but I'll get through it." • "What's the worst thing that could happen?" • "If I keep doing the same old thing, I'm only going to get more of the same."	
Word Descriptions	
• Movement • Heightened senses • Adrenaline • Consideration	• Warning • Protection • Seeking safety • Focusing inward

Skill 1: Clearly Define The Change

Sometimes there is a tendency to generalize your view or perception of change. For example, if people you work with are losing their jobs, it would be easy to call the change "people being laid off in the company." But look at it more clearly. That definition is really about a change for other people. Sure it might affect you, but pinpointing or defining what the change creates for you is the key. Your real change might be any of the following:

- My workload has doubled because of the layoffs.
- I must be prepared to be laid off since so many others have been.
- The layoffs have taken some of my closest friends away.

Notice that all the changes listed indicate a loss. Whatever losses are unresolved will hold us back from moving forward.

When we asked Jim what his losses were after the second accident, he said that being unable to compete as an athlete was a huge loss. He listed several others very quickly, which cued us into the fact that Jim was keenly aware of and in touch with the losses he had suffered. Because of his clarity, he could begin to focus in and work on defining each one separately. If Jim had tried all at once to deal with the big change of being a paraplegic, he would have been overwhelmed and most likely paralyzed emotionally, as well as physically.

By using the Change Cycle Locator™ self-assessment profile, you will be able to pinpoint the part of any change that is driving your thoughts, feelings, and behaviors. Once you know your bottom line issue, then you have defined your change and can begin the process of dealing with it in a healthy and real way.

Skill 2: Establish Desired Outcomes

What is an Outcome?

An outcome is a clear and specific statement of what I want if this change could turn out any way I desire. Outcomes then, are not so much goals to be achieved as they are a point on which to focus that is both compelling and motivating.

Successful Changers have an uncanny knack for immediately focusing on how they would like the change to turn out. They know how to create a compelling picture of the end result so that the immediate experience is more tolerable. This is a very resourceful way to deal with fear. *Successful Changers* know that, if you can imagine fears, then you can just as easily imagine a positive outcome.

As Jim dealt with his loss of competing in athletic events, he began to focus on his outcome of walking again. He told us that keeping that outcome in his mind all the time gave him the impetus to keep moving forward. It must be working, because after only nine months, Jim has already done what the doctors said couldn't happen; he has taken several steps!

Guidelines For Writing Outcomes

1. State what life would look or be like if the result of the change was exactly as you want it.
   What will you be doing?
   What will you be saying?
   What will you be feeling?
   What will you be thinking?
2. Make your picture compelling, realistic, and state it as if it is already true.
3. State how you will know when you have reached your outcome.
4. Specify when, how, and with whom you want the outcome.
5. Make sure your outcome is useful for yourself and for others.

Skill 3: Distinguish Between Real and Imagined Fears

As we have already mentioned, sometimes we fear things that, in the end, never happen or never turn out as bad as we thought they might. Unfortunately, by then, a lot of energy, panic, tears, ulcers, and who knows what else have been experienced. In Stage 1, there is plenty to be done without confusing your real fears with your imagined fears ones.

Real fears: Fears that have evidence to support them.

Imagined fears: Fears that we "make up" by imagining or projecting a negative experience.

Many of Jim's fears were very practical and very real. However, there is a great lesson here to learn from him. When the doctors suggested that he might never walk again, Jim began to search for different evidence. (That just goes to show that we have to be careful about allowing other people to plant fears in our minds.) He found other paraplegics who had learned to walk and he found some physical therapists who believed that it was possible, in his condition. With that real evidence, Jim decided to push the fear out of his mind and stay focused on his outcome to walk again. Obviously, these are fairly simple skills. But, the difference between *Successful Changers* and most of the rest of us is that they use them! You might as well get started now!

Congratulations for feeling safe enough to move forward to Stage 2!

Stage 1 Skills Building

1. *Refer to your results on the Change Cycle Locator™. What specific aspect of the change did you pinpoint to work on? Where are you on the Change Cycle™?*

2. *Using the guidelines for Skill 2, write a clear and concise outcome.*

3. *List your fears on a sheet of paper. Label each one, real or imagined. What can you do about the real fears?*

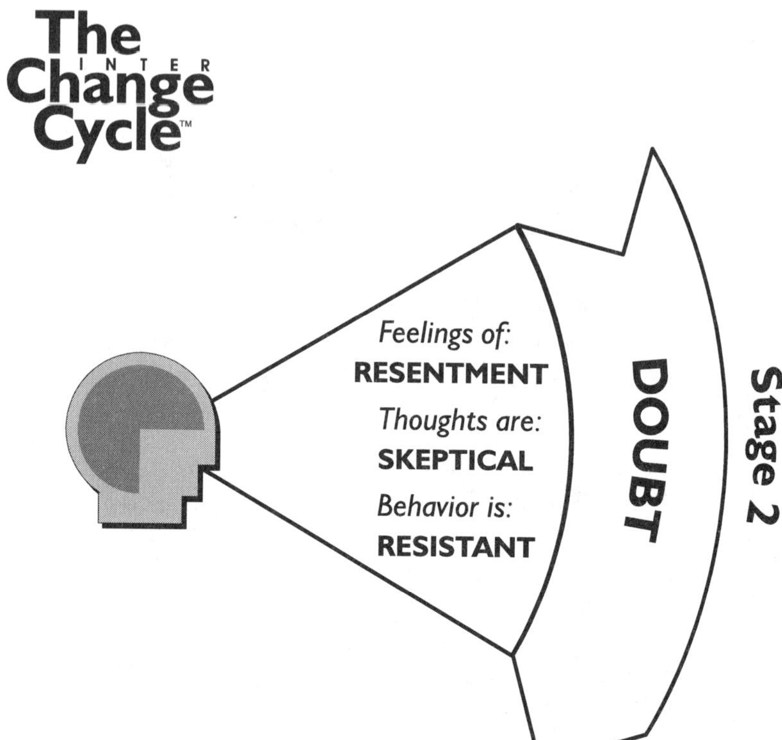

Stage 2—Me Against The Change	
Primary Experience:	Doubt
Major Focus:	Ego strength; being right
Stage Objective:	Gather accurate information
Motivated By:	Opinions or facts
Overuses:	Blaming self and others
Challenge:	Accepting valid information differing from your position
Opportunity:	Seeking and utilizing new knowledge

*"Ye shall know the truth,
and the truth shall make you mad"*

Aldous Huxley

Chapter 5

Me Against The Change

Stage 2: Doubt

As we enter Stage 2, we seem to naturally become more stubborn! Often referred to as "the loud Stage," this part of the process finds us firmly rooted in our own point-of-view and feeling a need to defend our position. Interestingly enough, we formulate our "position" based on a mixture of past experiences and current circumstances. While this is all our brain can deliver to us, we must remember that, at this juncture, we are missing some vital pieces of information.

It is only natural then, that we have an overwhelming sense of doubt. We doubt other people's motives, we doubt our own judgment, we doubt the outcome of the change, we doubt the validity of the reasons for the change, etc. So, having doubt is a great way for our brain to fill in the gaps of missing information. To doubt the change means resistance and skepticism are soon to follow. Once this happens, you may well be on your way to creating a negative hole filled with anger and resentment.

Gathering practical, useful and resourceful information is the way out of Stage 2. What if you choose to recognize doubt as a strategy for gathering information? What if we could understand doubt to be your brain's way of letting you know that you need to ask more questions? With the proper attitude, doubt can become a very powerful resource.

As you work with Stage 2, count it as one of the most important to master because it is where our attitude toward the change is created. That attitude can be good or bad. Choose well.

What Does Stage 2 Look Like?

Melissa, an attorney from Tampa, Florida, was in Los Angeles on business the day after the 1992 riots. After watching TV and hearing the warnings and the strict curfews, she was concerned for her safety. When she returned to the hotel after her first day of work, she stepped into the lobby elevator where three big and tall African-American men stood. Their faces were grave and somewhat unfriendly. Admittedly, she said she felt a bit nervous in light of all the unrest of the previous days. As the doors began to close, one of the men said, "Hit the floor." Melissa was terrified, but did what he said and dropped to her hands and knees. Then one of the men said, "Lady, he meant hit the floor you want to go to." Slowly, Melissa got up and feeling totally embarrassed, pressed her floor button. When the elevator finally stopped, she got out never looking back. Several days later when she went to check out, the clerk informed Melissa her bill had been taken care of. Melissa thought there must surely be some mistake and asked the clerk to check again. In a few minutes, he returned with a note that had been left for her. It said:

> *Taking care of your room was the least I could do. Thanks for the best laugh I've had in years.*
>
> Eddie Murphy

This is an excellent story for illustrating all the elements of Stage 2. Having approached her trip to Los Angeles with resistance, Melissa also took along a skeptical attitude.

How true it is that "things aren't always what they seem." As we discussed in Chapter 2, the operation of schema can often leave you with incomplete information. When Melissa received the note and combined that information with the experience in the elevator, her *schema* of the situation changed, became more complete. It was then possible for her to conclude that the men in the elevator were Eddie Murphy and his bodyguards. That explained for her why they looked "grave and unfriendly." Suddenly, the entire picture looked different. Never underestimate the power that the stored information in our brain has on our perception and, therefore, our behavior.

Feelings Of Resentment

Resentment in Stage 2 generally arises from the exhaustion of having to deal with the change at all. Whether we perceive the change to be good or bad, we still resent the pieces we'd rather not deal with. In Melissa's story, she never wanted to take the trip to Los Angeles during such a tenuous time and resented that she had to deal at all with her safety being put in jeopardy. On the upside, resentment then becomes a challenge because it will either motivate us to deal directly with the people and issues or, on the downside, it will create feelings of anger and bitterness that can take too much valuable time to eliminate.

RESENTMENT

Thoughts Are Skeptical

One of the most deceiving parts of Stage 2 is the effect skepticism has on us. We look around carefully and tend to question circumstances, as well as people. This skepticism sometimes causes us to formulate a point of view about the change that leads to an unwillingness to see all sides of the picture. Once we develop a "position" or point of view, we tend to spend a lot of time gathering information that will support our position.

The bad news about forming an opinion without adequate information is that the primary force or motivator becomes "being right" rather than "getting right". Once we lose our ability to get more information and see other perspectives, we have effectively lost our ability to accept new and accurate information; preventing us from to moving on to the next stage.

The good news is that a certain amount of skepticism can be a very useful resource. It should cause you to ask questions that will broaden your perspective and add to your overall knowledge and understanding of the change.

Behavior Is Resistant

It's not unusual to get into a fighting position and resist or defend ourselves against that which we perceive to be potentially threatening. However, it's important to remember that you are more than likely resisting the perception of a threat rather than the reality of a threat. Once we feel truly threatened by the change, we have the tendency to begin blaming ourselves and others as a way of resisting it.

Typically, blame is equally overused on both sides of the coin, blaming yourself and blaming others. Blaming can manifest itself as aggressive behavior, both passive and blatant. Additionally, thought patterns in Stage 2 are often defensive and focused on the lack of something, such as the lack of information, or the lack of having control over the change situation. This is a very dangerous point in the Change Cycle™ because it is the place where many people fail to take responsibility for themselves and/or their feelings and actions. Thus, nothing constructive is ever accomplished. As long as resistance, blame, and inaccurate information persist, very little resolution or forward movement is possible.

This can easily be seen in the social issues that face society today because of the conflict and controversy that surround them. When an issue becomes "significant", resistance to information and blame appear.

The following situation brings Stage 2 into clear view. The essence of the event occurred outside a Central Florida abortion clinic. The National Organization for Women (on the pro-choice side) and Operation Rescue (on the anti-abortion side) were picketing. The leaders of the two groups, angry over the issue, moved into the middle of the parking lot, drew a chalk line between them, and shouted angry words at one another for an hour.

Clearly, these groups were resisting and blaming one another in blatant ways, yet doing little to understand each other's position or gain any resolve or common ground. This becomes obviously silly when you consider the fact that both of these groups agree that abortion is a poor choice as a method for birth control. Admittedly,

Stage 2 can be played out more subtly and with less direct confrontation.

This kind of manifestation of blame and resistance can be very more damaging. This is because the resistance and blame are covert, manipulative and, very often, difficult to detect. They are covert because they distract you from the real issue or its facts. They are manipulative because they cause you to behave in such a manner as to prevent you from obtaining the information you need. They can be hard to detect because they hide behind other emotions such as hate, anger and resentfulness.

Here's an example. Marge was against her daughter, Terry, marrying Steve. Marge went through all the appropriate motions to prepare for the wedding, but certainly withheld her emotional support. Anytime Steve was around, she paid him little attention and avoided almost all verbal exchanges. For years, Marge has ignored her son-in-law and blamed her daughter for her feeling a lack of closeness. Even though the confrontation was subtle and quiet, it had a very destructive effect on her relationships because she was unwilling to resolve the change in her family.

Perhaps the most dangerous manifestation of Stage 2 is when the resistance and blame are turned inward. We see this very often with people who are overweight. Often times over weight people have difficulty in losing weight because they are unwilling or unable to see themselves any other way and resist any facts or information that suggest they really can do something about their weight. Some overweight people believe they don't deserve to be thin or they use their weight as a kind of symbolic protection from their inner self, their world, and their feelings. This is where the blame comes in. Until this pattern is broken and new information is allowed to enter, permanently losing their excess weight will be practically impossible.

The importance of resistant behavior is that it sends you a clear message to stop forward movement. Resistance means to hold back or pull away. When you notice you are being resistant, ask yourself these three questions. Why am I being resistant? Who am I resisting? What am I resistant of? Answering those questions will likely provide some missing pieces of relevant information that you need to successfully manage this part of the change.

When you resist and blame, it is very difficult to seek out or even be open to more information. In fact, there is a tendency to believe that information is deliberately being withheld or even to be satisfied with misinformation. Decide on what you need to know in order to be convinced that you have enough information. The tricky part of Stage 2 is remembering to stay focused on gaining information and formulating an accurate picture of the change. It is very easy to be lured toward resistance and blame. Be careful, because you may well find yourself very embarrassed if, after gathering information, you find that your resistance and blame were invalid.

Look at the behaviors and language patterns produced by the experience of doubt in the following table.

People Who Are Struggling With Doubt	
Behaviors	
• Defending your own position whether it is right or wrong • Being only able to see one perspective • Having a 'me versus them' or 'me versus the world' mentality • Being aggressive towards others	
Language Patterns	
• "I didn't . . . they did." • "I refuse to have someone else run my life." • "I don't like being forced into something." • "There's no way this could be the best thing for me."	
Word Descriptions	
• Defensive • Cynical • Obstinate • One-dimensional	• Angry • Blaming • Adversarial

What Do Successful Changers Do?

Successful Changer—Jerry Johnson

Jerry Johnson was sitting at the crossroads of his future. Even though he was only 17, he knew that it was time for some important choices to be made. He was internally motivated by his parents and his uncle's constant urging to seek out new possibilities and to value his schooling. Jerry could see the advantage of a college education, but had yet to make the commitment to use his high school years to prepare for that future.

The day he received his SAT scores for college admittance marked a change in Jerry's life that he still calls a catalyst today. He took those scores to his high school guidance counselor and asked her opinion about his college prospects. She looked at his scores, shook her head and suggested that he forget his college and career dreams and go find work in the town's battery factory. Jerry felt stabbed by her doubt. He had hoped for more, wanted more, expected more from himself, and yet this guidance counselor had dealt him a tough judgment.

Dejected, embarrassed, and depressed, Jerry shared his opinions with his father. Fearing his disappointment, Jerry was taken aback by his father's support and total belief in him. Jerry's father reminded him that no one person or event could ever predetermine his ability to achieve. He urged Jerry to make his own decisions about his future success and take action from that knowledge.

Jerry decided to pursue going to college and shared his dreams with one of his favorite teachers. When he hesitantly asked what the teacher thought, Jerry still can quote her response. "Jerry, just your coming to me shows that you have what it takes to be successful." That encouragement gave Jerry the momentum and motivation he needed to believe in himself. He made a personal commitment to his future and proved it by changing some of his priorities. His studies went to the top of the list, and sports and his social life were minimized. He says that keeping his eyes on the goal carried him through the dog days.

He did well in college and shortly after his graduation, he returned as a faculty member to his old high school. Guess whose boss he was? That's right, the guidance counselor who suggested he get a job at the factory. Life has a way of opening doors if we are willing to accept the changes.

Later, a career move to be an Assistant Manager for U.S. West Communications presented itself. Jerry again made a commitment to look at and plan for a new future. His new position provided opportunities that looked promising, and he strategically prepared to be ready for them.

In his 17 years at U.S. West, he has been promoted more times than anyone can remember and is known for assisting others with his encouragement and his support. Because he leads by example, he is a role model to others as they look to move ahead.

In January 1994, Jerry Johnson was named by *Black Enterprise Magazine* as one of the "Top Forty Most Powerful Black Executives in Corporate America." It was an honor to him and his company, but it was a surprise to no one. Jerry Johnson had decided a long time ago that by giving up his limitations he could allow success to fill those old spaces of doubt and fear.

Jerry's ability to turn his doubts into useful information gives us insight into the skills he and other *Successful Changers* use. The greatest lesson we can learn from *Successful Changers* in Stage 2 is this: If we formulate an accurate picture of the change and take responsibility for our reactions to that change, then we can be in charge of our own destiny.

Review the table. It shows the behavior and language patterns *Successful Changers* use to help themselves acquire new information.

People Who Are Successful Acquiring Information	
Behaviors	
• Asking questions; being open to the ideas of others • Holding a position while looking at the other side of a picture • Being methodical in acquiring new information or examining opinions • Respects valid information regardless of source	
Language Patterns	
• "Am I being fair to all concerned?" • "Do I really want to understand or do I just want my way?" • "How can I make things better?"	
Word Descriptions	
• Probing • Deliberate • Protective • Two-dimensional	• Careful • Insistent • Responsive

Successful Changers focus on three basic skills in Stage 2:

Skill 1: Reframe The Change

Reframing is changing a negative idea or statement into a positive one by changing the frame of reference by which you perceive the experience. There are different kinds of reframes, but in Stage 2 the most useful is called a *context reframe*. Context reframe means to think of a separate context or situation where you or someone else would respond differently to the same behavior.

For example, if you are very resentful toward someone else because they haven't given "the whole story" about the change, you might think, "It makes me angry and I resent the fact that he/she is withholding information." To reframe this sentence so that you are back in charge, think of a time when you had trouble getting information from someone else, but you did something that altered the situation so that you got what you needed. In doing so, you might say, "When I'm lost and someone gives me poor directions, I simply stop again and ask somebody else for the help I need. In my current situation, perhaps I should seek information from someone else."

With a little practice, context reframing will give you the ability to pull resources you've used successfully in the past into any present situation. Ultimately, this skill suggests that you have all the resources you need to move through any change. In essence, it is utilizing the information you already have in order to get the information you need! When Jerry Johnson's guidance counselor told him he was not college material, Jerry went to his father who reminded him that accepting other people's boundaries had never gotten them anywhere. So Jerry, with the help of his father, and a trusted teacher was able to be confident of overcoming other people's doubts. In doing so, he was able to take action rather than feel defeated.

Skill 2: Remember The Law of Cause and Effect

Everything you do, feel, or think (cause) has a result (effect). This is one of the most simple yet profound laws of the universe. Everything you do has a result or a consequence. It's like throwing a rock into a pond. There will be ripples. Some will be huge ripples, others medium, and others quite small. But they are all your ripples. You caused them by throwing the rock. So, when you look at the results in your life and don't like them, go back to the cause and take responsibility for changing it to get a better result. Likewise, if you like some of the results in your life, go back to the cause and take responsibility for continuing to do the things that have produced the effects you want.

Essentially, this principle states that you take responsibility for your actions, all of them. If you don't, who should? If something is happening to you that is aggravating or wonderful, stop and ask yourself this question: "What have I done to create this effect in my life?"

Is this easy? Not always. When your partner "snaps" at you for no apparent reason, it is difficult to stop and consider what you might have done to provoke such a response. It's much easier to blame or make them wrong. But, imagine what it would be like if both of you were willing to operate by a sense of responsibility when you have a misunderstanding. Instead of defending your position, you both would be evaluating what you did that contributed to the conflict rather than blaming the other person. This is an attitude of "solution finding" instead of "problem solving". This is an excellent way to stay in control of your own life. After all, if it's always someone else's fault when things go wrong, whose fault is it when things go right? When are you in charge? Why?

Is his book, *People of the Lie*, M. Scott Peck concludes that people aligned with evil have a glaring characteristic of never taking responsibility for any of their actions; they always see themselves as victims. Conversely, we find that *Successful Changers* consider the principle of cause and effect (taking responsibility) their creed. Because they do, they are willing and able to gather valuable information about themselves that sheds light on the overall situation.

We asked Jerry Johnson how he took responsibility for the situation that caused his SAT scores to be low and, therefore, produced the effect of his counselor recommending he not attend college. Jerry told us that he realized in that moment that he must change his focus by giving up some things in order to focus on his priorities. His willingness to do so eventually gave him the grades he needed to get into college.

Skill 3: Gathering Information That Creates An Accurate Picture

During Stage 2, any information being gathered is usually for the purpose of supporting your position. However, *Successful Changers* know that in order to move forward, they must pull together the information that will give them an accurate picture of what the change really entails. Defending a position becomes unimportant while having accurate information becomes vital. It would be useful to stop and think about a time when you did a good job of gathering information. Perhaps it was when you bought a car, a new house, or your stereo. Maybe it was when you hired a new employee, found a new babysitter, or picked which college you would attend. Remember how good it felt to have all the information you could find.

The truth of the matter is that whatever event you just remembered constituted some sort of change you were attempting to make. This goes to prove that there have been times when you traveled through Stage 2 effectively. Remember this the next time you're tempted to be upset simply because you are operating on incomplete or inaccurate information.

When Jerry Johnson went to a trusted teacher to get

feedback about his ability to succeed in college, the teacher told him he had what it takes to be successful. What if Jerry had failed to seek out more information? His life today might be different!

Again, notice how simple these skills are. Hopefully, you're making an even greater commitment to practice them. They're all within your reach!

Now that you have learned more about the red Stages, 1, Loss and 2, Doubt, it should be easy to see that they are very important and are ultimately positive because they provide safety and information about the change. Keep in mind that you always have a choice. You can get caught up in defensive positioning that will lead to denial or do what it takes to maintain your safety and an accurate picture so you can continue your forward progress.

With these new skills, you are ready to move to Stage 3!

Stage 2 Skills Building

1. *Consider what you are resisting the most in the change you are facing. What do you need to know to help you deal with this part of the change?*

2. *Think of a recent conflict you've had with another person. As you reflect on it, write down the things you may have done to contribute to the conflict. What did you do to assist in its resolution? What could you have done differently or better?*

3. *Take time to consider what information is missing for you in this change. Who or what can fill in the gaps?*

If you must assume something,
assume that there is something
you don't know.

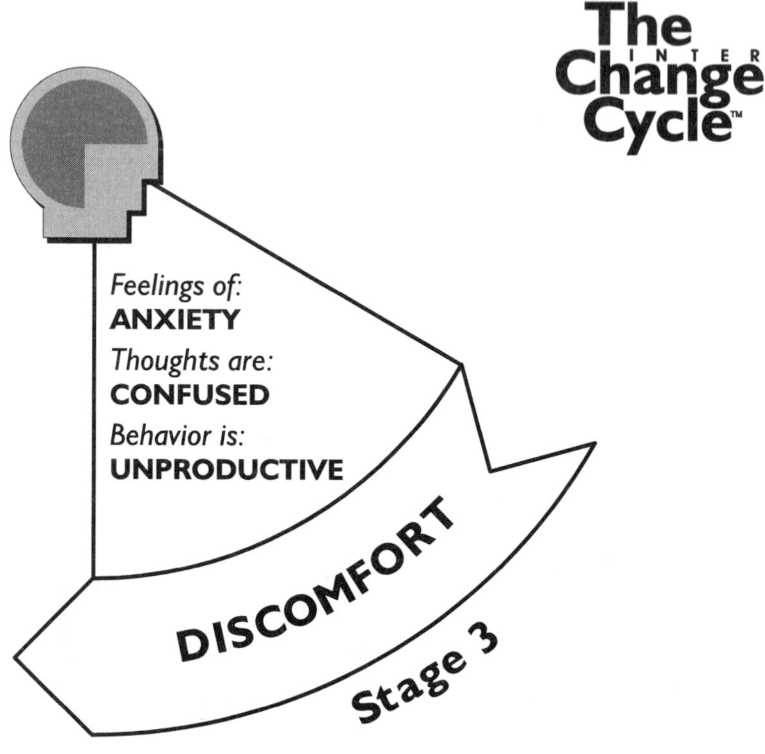

Stage 3—The Change And Me	
Primary Experience:	**Discomfort**
Major Focus:	**The "problem"**
Stage Objective:	**Self-motivation**
Motivated By:	**Impatience or possibility**
Overuses:	**Being overwhelmed**
Challenge:	**Keeping anxiety from becoming depression**
Opportunity:	**In the midst of chaos, learning to take small, breakthrough steps**

"Reality is the leading cause of stress among those who are in touch with it."

Jane Wagner

Chapter 6

The Change And Me

Stage 3: Discomfort

Stage 3 is known as the *breakthrough* or *breakdown* place. If you think about the imagery of the title of this Chapter, "The Change And Me," you'll see that it is as though you are walking side-by-side with the change, yet keeping it at arm's length. Certainly this means that you have made progress because you are facing in the same direction as the change. For the first time in the process, you have a real opportunity to do the things that will bring the change into your world, rather than seeing it as something separate. Conversely, it is also the stage that can trip you up and cause the entire process to break down.

Having completed Stage 2, you have gathered enough information to be clear about what the change really looks like and what it really means. Essentially, you have created a new schema that is more accurate than the one you used in the beginning of the process. In many ways, there is relief with this new picture. Many of the issues you assumed to be negative turn out to be different (and better) than you imagined. Some of the issues you thought were real, turned out to be things you made up in your own mind. The need to be angry and blame others has subsided since there is a better understanding of the true picture. There is a greater sense of security in knowing what the reality surrounding the change is.

However, with this new reality comes a fair amount of discomfort. It is much like breaking in a new pair of shoes. You buy the shoes knowing you like how they look, how well they fit, and what they cost. What you bought is clear, but the shoes still hurt your feet until you break them in. During this initial period of discomfort, it is frustrating that any shoes that look so good could hurt so bad. Then one day, all of a sudden, the pain goes away. The shoes feel fine. Your feet are happy. Life is good.

Stage 3 is like breaking in new shoes. Even though the picture is clear, it is accompanied by anxiety, confusion, and low productivity. The combination of these experiences can either produce stress that causes breakdown or can be channeled to produce determination that creates a breakthrough, allowing you to move forward.

What Does Stage 3 Look Like?

In Stage 3, when the picture of the change gets some clarity, it is often frustrating and less than what you hoped for. When this reality sets in, it is essential that you be aware of what is happening in and around you.

Diana Nyad was more than an Olympic athlete, she was as determined about her life as she was her swimming. One remarkable physical accomplishment led to another. Her mark in the sport of swimming will forever be honored.

The misty, grey morning when she entered the cold, choppy water to swim across the English Channel Diana felt anxious, yet determined. Because her conditioning had been so good, Diana was making good time and swimming strong. But as the hours went on and the pain slowly began to throb through her body, she began to lose some of her momentum. Diana's coach was in a boat next to her monitoring the water conditions and keeping her on the right path. The salt water had caused her lips to swell and blister and the cold temperature of the water was adding to the severity of her muscle cramps. Her coach had become seriously worried and encouraged her to please get out of the water; to quit and try again another time.

Diana had become disoriented because of her pain and fatigue and had lost all orientation of where she was in relation to the perspective of finishing. Trusting of her coach, but frustrated at the prospect of quitting, Diana struggled with her choices. Finally the fog in her mind as well as the fog surrounding her in the water, led her to give in. As she huddled in a blanket in the boat, Diana realized that she had been less than 1 mile from the shore. One mile! Through the fog she had lost sight of her goal and let the circumstances get the better of her. Diana admitted later that under any condition she physically could swim one mile. Her disappointment was overwhelming.

Unfortunately, in Stage 3, it is easy to allow anxiety, confusion and low productivity to fog your view of what is ahead. Remember Diana's story and keep swimming, because you are very close to the shore.

Feelings Of Anxiety

As the reality of the change sets in, it is natural that a certain amount of anxiety is likely to follow. Since Stage 3 presents to you the new challenge of a clear picture, and the responsibility of assimilating it into your current circumstances, you are likely to worry about how this is going to affect you. The good news is in a real day-to-day sense, anxiety is nothing more than worrying about something that might happen in the future. On the other hand, this can be a trap because your feelings of anxiety are pro-

duced by your mind's concern over the worst possible outcome. After all, if your mind was worrying about the best possible outcome, you would never call it "anxiety," you'd call it "excitement" or anticipation. The major characteristic to notice about anxiety is that you are making up scenarios about the future (that or often negative) that may or may not come true. Here's a thought, since you're making them up anyway, why not make up positive scenarios that leave you in a more resourceful and powerful state of mind?

Thoughts Are Confused

Mental chaos is commonly referred to as confusion. Your brain is working hard to sort through information and deliver it to your conscious mind in a usable format. That is learning. Can you remember a time during a junior high school math class when you went for days feeling confused about a particular type of problem, and then suddenly something clicked and you knew the sequence of steps and how to get the answer. Many of us (OK, some of us) experienced that with multiplication tables. One day the brain is mud, the next day, brilliant.

Confusion may make you think that you're "stupid" or "crazy" or "slow" because you're struggling to make sense of all the new information and stimulation. This is particularly true if there are other people around who seem to have it all figured out. Another challenge is that of being overwhelmed with thoughts of how to do all the things you had on your plate before the change came along, and add to it, all the things required by the change. When the brain is in overload you begin thinking in circles. It may become difficult to complete even the simplest tasks. Not to worry. A great thinker (I'm confused as to which one) once said, confusion is the final step before learning. We all hope so.

Behavior Is Unproductive

Low productivity eventually increases the level of anxiety and confusion, which can create a vicious circle of frustration. This frustration serves as such a major distraction that even the everyday tasks that used to be easy to complete, become difficult. It also creates feelings of low self-esteem because of the seeming inability you have to get anything done.

Stage 3 at its worst means the body begins to show signs of stress and depression. The most common symptoms are shoulder and neck tension, stomach problems, and general lethargy. These physical messages are an indicator of the mind-body connection. When anxiety and confusion are part of our daily experience, they eventually express themselves in the body. Even mild stress can add to your inability to be productive and full of energy, while deep stress can have serious mental, emotional, and physical complications.

As you can see, Stage 3 can be overwhelming. With these multi-dimensional experiences happening simultaneously, they are very often misinterpreted. Be aware of the symptoms and know your cures for anxiety, confusion, and low productivity. Recognizing the problem is half the battle. Doing something about it is the other half.

One of the things you can do is to look more closely at how you may be allowing anxiety, confusion and low productivity to control you. Consider the ways you might turn that around. For example:

Anxiety—means we are worrying about something that hasn't happened yet. If it hasn't happened, then we can take charge of it and create a different outcome.

Confusion—means that we are in an ideal state to learn something new and useful. The brain is processing and creating a pathway for new knowledge. If you understand enough to be "confused," you are assimilating new learnings.

Low Productivity—means that the body and mind are out of sync with one another. As we take charge of our own outcomes and become more open to learning, the body will follow suit with added energy and/or needed relaxation.

Now that you can recognize the signs of Stage 3, it is important to stay focused on your need for motivation. Motivation will provide the energy, the push (or the pull) when you are in the doldrums. *Successful Changers* know that taking action and staying in motion are the keys to moving through Stage 3. They teach us that if there is mental action and physical action, the emotional shifts will follow.

Look at the behaviors and language patterns produced by the experience of discomfort in the following table.

People Who Are Struggling With Discomfort	
Behaviors	
• Being non-participative • Being wishy-washy; not being able to commit • Being rude to others • Being unable to prioritize • Being disorganized • Being slow to respond to needs or requests of others	
Language Patterns	
• "I don't care." • "There's no use, why bother." • ". . . Whatever."	
Word Descriptions	
• Uncaring • Temperamental • Unresponsive • Cranky • Overwhelmed	• Tired • Selfish • Lethargic • Puzzled • Worried

What Do Successful Changers Do?

Successful Changer—John Box

John Box was a California kind of guy. He loved the beach, his friends, and his motorcycle. Life was good. He was riding his motorcycle when on November 1, 1981, a car pulled in front of him and he went down. As John skidded across the pavement and under a truck, his motorcycle followed and landed on top of him. It took two hours to free his body. Three times the rescue crew thought they had lost him. After five months of therapy he went home as a paraplegic.

John had lived through severe physical, mental, and emotional trauma, and it changed his life forever. John's body was functioning at a different level, but his mind longed for something to "do." Everybody told him to get a degree in computers. Because he was in a wheelchair, that's what he should do. That was a change to his original plan, but he said okay, for a while. Then John began to choose the changes. Computers were great, but he wanted something more and he switched to study metallurgical engineering. Next he started a business with his brother manufacturing tooling equipment for the aerospace industry. They were very successful.

Then the times changed. Defense contracts were drying up and John saw an opportunity to change the scope of his business by using his skills and technology in metallurgy to design and build a new lightweight, yet very durable wheelchair for active people with disabilities. John's creative signature to these sporty wheelchairs was the addition of colors, lots of colors. Any colors you could want. Colors N' Motion was born. "It was a radical and very satisfying change to go from making tools for bombs and fighter jets to a personalized industry where we really cared about our customers' needs," John explained. "We build our wheelchairs according to what the customer wants. Our youngest customer so far is eight years old and the oldest, seventy-three. Our wheelchairs help them stay active." They are helping John stay active, too. He is a serious athlete and a champion tennis and basketball player. "I love seeing our chairs in the winner's circle!"

Sometimes it takes a while to assimilate all of the changes that can happen at once. John Box didn't know what it meant to be paralyzed and he had no concept of what being a paraplegic would actually mean. Life had dealt him a change card he hadn't planned on. Wheelchairs were nowhere in his future plan. Now they are one of his gifts to the world, not just for his world, but for the world of many people with disabilities.

"When I was in the hospital, trying to learn how I was going to live again, my doctor told me to look at my life like a mountain. I was at the home base of the mountain and I couldn't get any lower. Because of my paralysis, maybe my mountain was a little steeper than some, but I knew I had to climb it. I knew that whatever came up, I could handle it. When I finally got to the top of the mountain, I looked out and guess what I saw—other mountains! Life is like that."

Obviously, John Box understands change. As a paraplegic and an entrepreneur, John and Colors N' Motion have become a company that can motivate others to change their lifestyle, and sometimes their outlook. This California-kind-of-guy cycled through the changes life sent him, but some things remain the same — he loves the beach, his wife, his friends, and his company. John Box is on a roll.

Successful Changers use these behaviors and language patterns to help motivate themselves to change.

People Who Are Successful With Motivation	
Behaviors	
• Working with others to solve problems • Taking steps to commit • Looking for motivation through opinion sharing, using books, tapes, etc. • Being able to set priorities • Cleaning up and organizing • Taking time out for fun, exercise, or a change of pace or scenery	
Language Patterns	
• "Hey what about me?" • "I can't stand this anymore, I'm going to do something different." • "I'm tired of this, I'm moving on." • "Anything is better than this."	
Word Descriptions	
• Perseverance • Tenacious • Impatient • Courageous	• Questioning • Determined • Persistent • Probing

The following *Successful Changer* skills can keep you moving in the right direction.

Skill 1: Take Mental Action

Getting "stuff" out of your head and writing your thoughts and feelings on paper will significantly ease your stay in Stage 3. Some of the frustrations of this stage are created because so many thoughts are swimming around and around in our heads. It's easy to think things are worse than they really are. Commit yourself to "working it all out" by simply taking a piece of paper and making two columns. Label one thoughts and the other feelings. Write whatever comes up for you in the appropriate column. Having this information will assist you in being realistic about what specifically is going on inside you.

Another part of mental action is that of renaming the things that are happening in your mind and body, and with your emotions. This is a form of reframing called *meaning reframes*. Specifically, this renaming is the process of changing the meaning of a negative emotion such as anxiety, confusion or lethargy into an emotion that is more positive or more resourceful. Here is an example:

Behavior: I am so tired all the time. I must be coming down with a cold.

Reframe: I am so tired all the time. I need to revitalize my energy by having fun and doing something I really enjoy.

It is a human tendency to attach some kind of meaning to our experiences. More often than not, the meaning attached is negative. If the power is ours to attach a meaning, why not make the meaning useful, resourceful, and positive? You have nothing to lose by doing reframes every day. It can be one of the most powerful and healthy habits you'll ever have!

John Box looked at "the mountain" as an obstacle and his doctor assisted him in reframing by attaching a meaning that caused John to believe he could climb it!

Skill 2: Create Mental Distraction

Most of us are prone to think that when we're having trouble getting tasks done and have fallen behind, (low productivity) the last thing we can do is take time out to relax or have fun. After all, if we stay at it and keep trying to get something finished or accomplished, sooner or later we might catch up. Unfortunately, activity doesn't necessarily produce results, especially in Stage 3. *Successful Changers* know that they can easily double their output if they will stop and set meaningful priorities by eliminating the distractions and busy work. They know focused energy creates momentum.

Distract your conscious, "worrying" mind by doing "out of the ordinary" or "relaxing" activities. Some of the greatest awarenesses come when you are relaxed.

Here are some easy ideas:

- Drive to work a new way.
- Read a type of book you've never read before.
- Try a new restaurant.
- Have a treat that you usually deny yourself.
- Have a "fun" night out with your friends.
- Go see a funny movie.
- Play games with your kids.
- Work in the yard.
- Play pinball or computer games.
- Watch four silly sitcoms in a row.
- Call an old friend you haven't talked to in years.

John Box returned to sports to distract himself from his new body. The distraction of tennis and basketball led to his new business and a new lease on life.

Skill 3: Commit To Physical Action

Since Stage 3 has thoughts, behaviors, and emotions that are intense and can cause mild symptoms of depression, pay special attention to the effect they have on your body. Body movement, mental action, and shifting your flow of energy are all things that will make you feel better in Stage 3. Unfortunately, because of anxiety, confusion, and low productivity, we are less likely to do the very things that would help. No matter how bad your body feels, physical action of any kind will help immediately. Here are a few ideas:

1. Relieve your physical stress. Take a mental and emotional "time-out" by giving your body some special

attention. Getting a massage, sitting in the jacuzzi, or a warm bubble bath are excellent ways to relax the body.

2. Replenish and nourish your body. Breath is the very essence of life. When our bodies and minds are lethargic, breathing tends to be shallow. This means that our organs and cells are deprived of the oxygen they need to keep them vital and energetic. Feeling low? Take five very deep breaths, sending the air down to your toes and exhaling from your ankles. Be prepared for a quick burst of physical and mental energy.
3. Move your body! While in Stage 3, it is helpful to be with other people, so do some exercise, preferably activity that involves at least one other person: golf, tennis, softball, basketball, aerobics, jogging/walking with a partner, bowling, swimming, cutting the grass, washing the car with your kids.

Give yourself permission to do something you enjoy that involves movement of some kind. These things don't have to be formal exercise, they only have to support you in giving your body an opportunity to stay active. Think of some things you really enjoy doing that are not classified as exercise, but do create activity for your body. Here are some examples:

- Shopping
- Visiting museums
- Walking on the beach
- Picnicking in the park
- Camping
- Having a party
- Play with your pets

Perhaps when you get lax about wanting to exercise your body, it would be good to remember that, even in a wheelchair, John Box plays basketball and tennis. He'd be the first to tell you that physical release means stress release.

Congratulations on your breakthrough! The hardest part is over and Stage 4 will be a welcome relief and an energizing adventure.

Are you getting the picture? With a little practice, you will be a *Successful Changer* too! The following exercises will polish your new Stage 3 skills.

Stage 3 Skills Building

1. *Take a few minutes and write down every little thing you feel responsible, nagged, or compelled to do. Forget order and categories and priorities. Just write. Simply get it out of your head. You are creating the biggest and most comprehensive to-do list of your life.*

   Whew! Now that they are all on paper, you can decide which ones you are going to do, and which to ignore. (No guilt, please!)

2. *Think of the last time you felt totally relaxed. Allow yourself to go back and remember how good your body felt, how peaceful your thoughts were and how your energy affected your mood. Get in a comfortable position and by remembering that time transport yourself back there and feel the relaxation.*

3. *What is one activity you can do that is both fun and will offer your body movement and regeneration? When will you do it?*

The INTER Change Cycle™

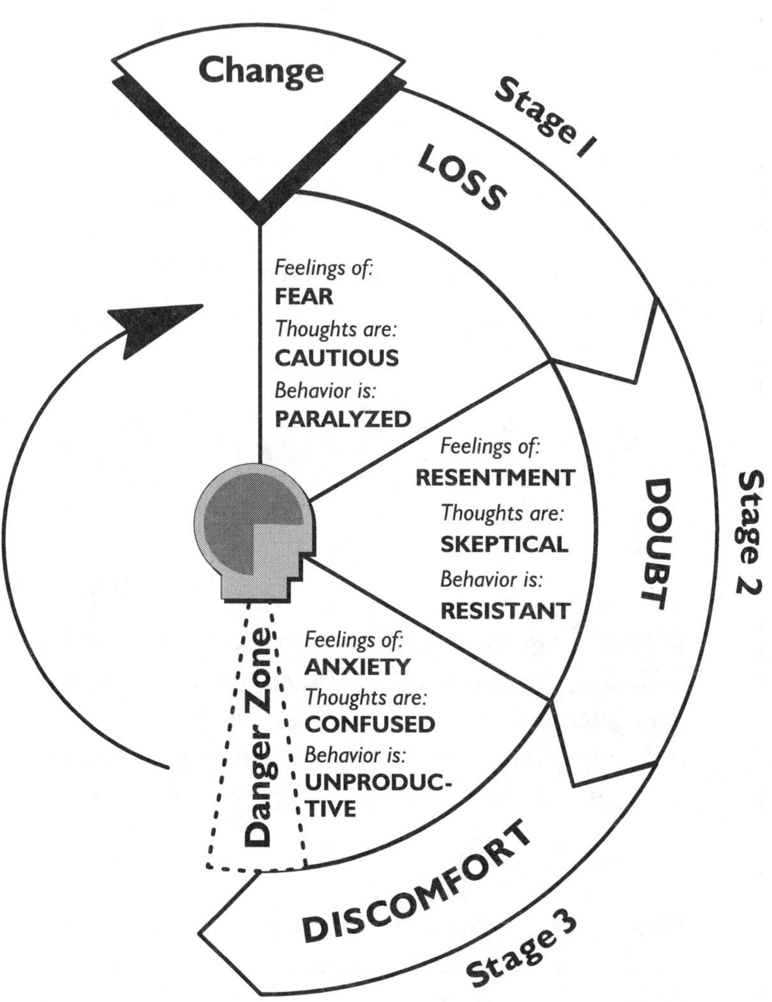

The Danger Zone

"If we open a quarrel between the past and the present, we shall find that we have lost the future."

Winston Churchill

Chapter 7

The Danger Zone

There was a time when jewelry boxes were equipped with weapons that could kill anyone who attempted to rob them without knowing the secret to gain entrance and acquire the jewels. One such jewelry case, sold at an auction in New York, stood about fourteen inches high by twenty inches wide and ten inches deep. It had a bottom lock for the jewelry drawer and a secret top lock for the weapons. If the bottom lock for the jewelry drawer was tampered with before the top lock of the weapons was disarmed, four doors instantly flew open, pistols sprang into position and fired automatically. Understandably, this is one theory of where the term, "Pandora's Box", originated.

When you reach Stage 3 in the Change Cycle™, you are staring at the possibility of passing into The Danger Zone. If you do, it is much like playing with the loaded jewelry box.

You now have an opportunity to be fully aware of the existence of The Danger Zone so that you are never surprised. You can easily avoid it, once you know what's necessary to move past it. Notice that, on the Change Cycle™ model, The Danger Zone never breaks the plane of the outside ring. This visually represents:

- Staying in Stage 3 too long leads to The Danger Zone.
- Moving from Stage 3 to Stage 4 along the outside ring ensures a safe passage.

The Danger Zone is between Stages 3 and 4 because this is the point of turning the corner to a more pleasurable part of the change process or looping back to Stage 1 and starting over. Because most people have no awareness about how the change process works, it is easy to get stuck and then continually loop back through Stages 1, 2, and 3. Of course, this means that the successful completion of any change rarely happens for some people. No wonder change is considered a "negative" or "uncontrollable" experience by some people. Change success has eluded them. In many ways, moving beyond The Danger Zone is the key to a whole new experience of change.

Recognizing The Danger Zone

In the interest of acknowledging what is called "reality," there is the possibility that you may at times land in The Danger Zone. It is like a big slide. You start in Stage 3 and then slide down back into Stage 1. Remember the game

Chutes and Ladders? If you slide back down to Stage 1, what you need is a ladder to climb back up. Avoiding the Danger Zone is not the issue, getting out of it quickly, is!

Much like the four pistols in the jewelry box, there are four dangers that will be facing you at The Danger Zone. Knowing how to respond to each of them is the key to moving forward and through the zone. Let's look at the four dangers and see what strategies you need to move quickly to Stage 4 instead of looping back to Stage 1 and having to start all over again.

Danger 1: The Overwhelming Urge To Give Up

When the confusion and anxiety of Stage 3 are present for too long, you may have the urge to throw your hands in the air and say, "forget it." At this juncture, walking away from it all becomes the focus. This attitude of denial will send you right back to Stage 1. Sometimes the grass is greener on the other side of the fence, sometimes it's worse. Put things in their proper perspective. Take a step back and look at the bigger picture. What else is going on that you hadn't noticed before?

Action Strategy:

Give your time, money, energy, and caring to someone less fortunate than you. This should give your circumstances a different perspective.

Reconsider, re-focus, and motivate yourself to keep moving forward!

Danger 2: Picturing Yourself As Useless or Hopeless

When you allow yourself to have prolonged low productivity, the result is a progressive feeling of uselessness often followed by hopelessness. The more you fail to complete tasks or accomplish goals, the more your self-esteem suffers. Take action quickly to get out of this spiral.

Action Strategy:

Think of just one thing you can do really well. Keep it simple. Maybe you know how to work your VCR. Tape a video for a friend. Or make a music tape. Bake some cookies to take to work. Send a 'no occasion' card to a friend or family member. Re-arrange your furniture. Organize the closet. Start something. Finish something. Reap the rewards! Who could benefit from that skill or gift? A child? A senior citizen? A hospital? Go now and offer it. Do a great job and really internalize the appreciation and compliments you will receive.

Danger 3: Believing That You Can Cover Up The Pain

One of the most damaging things to the human mind and body is that of covering up your pain. This offers the delusion that the pain is gone, but in reality, it intensifies. If being in Stage 3 too long is causing you pain, it can lead to depression. Face it head-on. In the long run you will save yourself a lot of heartaches. Get help now!

Action Strategy:

Find someone (a friend, counselor, family member, pastor) you can talk to. Tell them the truth, let them help. It's far too difficult to ask yourself all the right questions and come up with all the right answers alone. Right? Right!

Danger 4: Believing That You Are Working Hard For Nothing

Sometimes in the midst of high anxiety, it is possible to lose sight of the ultimate purpose. In fact, anxiety is always about the future so that means you are making up and focusing on a possible negative outcome. If you can make up a negative one, why not make a positive outcome by inserting anticipation into your future? Revisit the outcome you worked on earlier as a way of gaining perspective. This will help you to focus on the good reasons for working hard. Make this shift now!

Action Strategies:

Ask yourself these questions:

- What would happen if I could stop the process of this change?
- What would happen if I didn't stop the process and went forward with the change?
- What wouldn't happen if I did stop the process of this change?
- What wouldn't happen if I didn't stop the change process and went forward?

After writing the answers to these questions, focus on what you have to gain by sticking with the change at hand.

Avoiding The Danger Zone

One of the tricky parts of Stage 3 is to avoid The Danger Zone altogether. If you notice that you're beginning to slip backward toward Stage 2 (blame and resistance) in your feelings and behavior, let that be a signal that "going backward" has become your coping mechanism. Should you notice that you have lost your sense of humor, create opportunities to laugh and by all means, take yourself and others more lightly. As you might well imagine, this part of the Change Cycle™ can be difficult especially because Stage 3 affects your clarity of thought, your physical energy, and your ability to complete tasks. Getting to Stage 4 will be the light at the end of a long, dark tunnel.

There are five steps that can help you to steer clear of The Danger Zone.

Step 1.
Be aware of the location of The Danger Zone.

This may sound trite, but the most common factor for landing in the middle of The Danger Zone is the failure to anticipate its presence in the process. Remember the jewelry box. For those who knew the secret of the hidden weapons, there was no element of surprise. They knew how to avoid the guns and what to expect if the top lock was tampered with.

Action Strategy:

As you approach The Danger Zone, remain very aware of the warning signs and the cost of looping back to Stage 1 and starting over. Take some time now to write down the consequences of your looping back through the first three stages. Is this a pattern for you? Are you ready to risk it?

Step 2.
Increase your physical activity.

It is a fact that anxiety, confusion, and low productivity (Stage 2) can cause mild depression. Unchecked depression leads to more depression. It never has to come to that, but doing things that drive away depression are essential. The most simple and effective way is increased physical activity. Making this decision may seem difficult when you are feeling down and have low energy, but you must, sometimes by sheer force of will. It is particularly important to do activities outdoors. Exposure to fresh air, sunlight, water, and the Mother earth below your feet feeds the body and nurtures the soul in a way nothing else can!

Action Strategies:

Taking a walk or working in the yard can relieve stress and renew vitality. The tension you've brought on by the change must be released from the body because otherwise, the body can wear down and, in some cases, become sick. It would be great if you would do cardiovascular exercise at least three times per week. This routine strengthens the heart and relieves tension. Before starting any vigorous exercise plan, it is always best to check with your doctor. Remember, any time you can take a walk or do some simple exercise, you will be increasing the speed of your body's metabolism which will work to release your tensions and allow your body to assist you. Here are a few examples of lifestyle exercises that are very easy to engage in:

- Park further away from your office or the mall and walk at a fast pace to your destination.
- Go walking with a friend and do all your complaining as you walk.
- Use stairs whenever they are available instead of elevators, escalators, or moving sidewalks.

Another excellent form of exercise for all ages is to become involved in one of the martial arts. Start by signing up for a six-week class and go from there. Tai Chi and Aikido are particularly helpful because they teach specific concepts that will reduce stress. In most martial arts, you will learn how to be centered, balanced, and how to flow with energy instead of against it. You will quickly find these skills a priceless support to your well-being.

Step 3.
Stay committed to and focused on the Stage 3 tools.

Successful Changers almost never find themselves in The Danger Zone because they stay so focused on getting to Stage 4. They do "whatever it takes" to get them there easily and with minimum wear and tear on their nerves.

Action Strategy:

Go back to the Stage 3 tools and skills and pick your favorite. Write down how you can use this skill or tool to expedite your movement to Stage 4.

Step 4.
Find a "Change Partner" who is committed to encouraging you and supporting you in moving forward.

When The Danger Zone is looming, it is easy to be drawn to people who feel as bad as you do. Unfortunately, these people will only support you in feeling worse. Remember this:

> *Everyone is supporting you for something! Make sure the people you are surrounded by are supporting you for the life you really want to live.*

One of the best ways to get positive support is to choose a "change partner." This is someone who believes that you can change successfully. This might mean supporting you in a variety of areas, such as looking for a new job or career, attaining your ideal weight, or adjusting to your new life after the children leave home. The key is to have a partner that will stay focused on your goal even when you're not.

Action Strategy:

Since Stage 3 and The Danger Zone tempt us to lose all sense of structure and discipline, it is a good idea to formalize the "change partner" relationship. That means, set up a regular time to meet and agree on specific things you will do and/or discuss to support one another when you are together.

Sample Change Partner Meeting:

- Meeting once each week gets the best results.
- Review with each other where you think you are in the Change Cycle™.
- Go over the tools for that Stage. Celebrate the victories you've had in this area.
- Share with each other which tools you need some support in utilizing better.
- Offer support to each other by encouraging your partner and believing in their ability to do whatever needs to be done.
- Agree to touch base with one another at least once before your next meeting.

The real benefit of this practice is that you consistently focus on your ability to be a *Successful Changer*. In doing so, over time, you will be able to make changes for yourself that you never thought possible. This will lead to powerful results! Dare yourself and do it now!

Step 5.
Master the skill of creating "Meaning Reframes."

You have already learned to do reframing and perhaps have even written a few reframes that you are using regularly. Now it's time to practice formulating them on the spot. In this particular phase of the change process, meaning reframes are the most helpful. This is because you have a propensity here to take in new information and experiences and attach the worst possible meaning to them.

Action Strategy:

It is an absolute must that you train yourself to be aware and immediately reframe negative thoughts and feelings into positive and productive feelings, thoughts, and behaviors.

Meaning Reframe Examples

1. "I am so angry that traffic is backed up and I'm going to be late."

   Reframe:

   "Maybe my being stuck in this traffic is keeping me out of an accident that I otherwise might have been involved in."

2. "I am so tired of being confused."

   Reframe:

   "Since I'm so thoroughly confused, I must be on the brink of a breakthrough!"

3. "My stomach hurts almost all of the time."

Reframe:

My body is communicating to me that I need to relieve stress and take care of myself. "

4. I don't have enough time to do everything that is expected of me right now!"

   Reframe:

   "Having all these things to do must be a message that I need to be more aware of all the resources available to me. I must learn to say no!"

Admittedly, this takes practice, but the results are worth it. Reframing is easy and it will support you in seeing the world in a much more resourceful way.

As you can see, The Danger Zone gets its name honestly. It is no fun. But now you have everything you need to stay out, or move through it quickly. The extra work and focus will be worth it! Stage 4 means you've turned the corner. You're ready now to begin experiencing the change process and yourself in a creative and productive way.

"If you are going through Hell,
keep going."

Winston Churchill

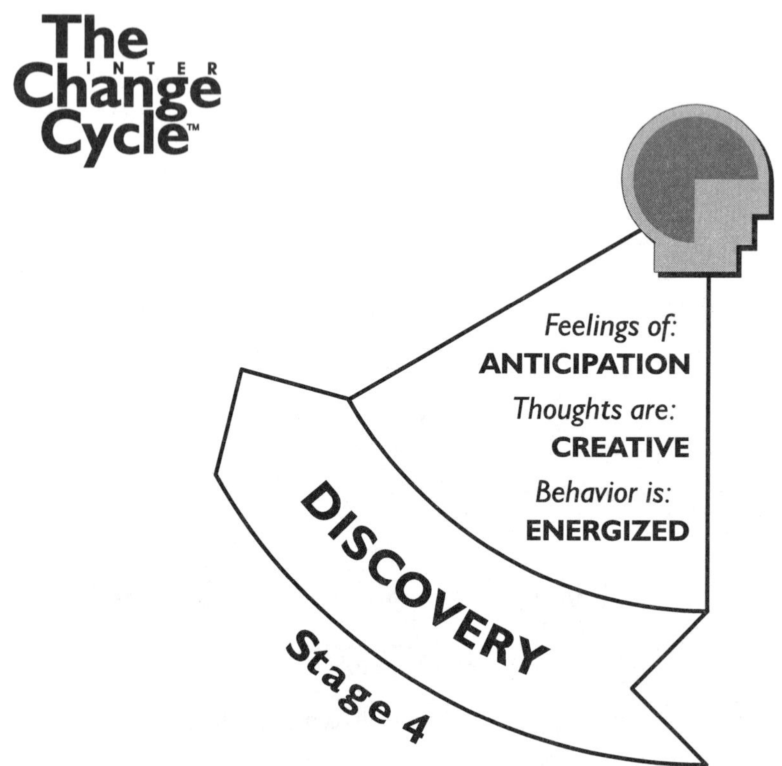

Stage 4—Me Becoming The Change	
Primary Experience:	**Discovery**
Major Focus:	**The solutions**
Stage Objective:	**Making decisions from available options**
Motivated By:	**Frustration or multiple choices**
Overuses:	**Enthusiasm**
Challenge:	**Acting on your decisions**
Opportunity:	**Knowing how to keep focused on the priorities**

"If you need a helping hand, you'll find one at the end of your own arm."

Yiddish Proverb

Chapter 8

Me Becoming The Change

Stage 4: Discovery

As you enter Stage 4, you are still in a yellow stage which is a sign that there are still issues that must be assimilated, so caution is in order. In Stage 3, you were assimilating information and attempting to make sense of the "change" that still existed outside of you. In Stage 4, the change has internalized and you begin integrating information in a new way because of your new perspective.

This new shift in perspective dramatically enhances your ability to seek and identify with others about the change. Internalization of the change allows you to offer yourself to the change as a partner for success instead of fighting and resisting it as an adversary or enemy.

Kaleidoscopes provide an interesting study in 'perspective'. In most speciality gift shops, a wide variety of styles and sizes are available. If you watch, people young and old, play with them. They become mesmerized as they look at the wonderful array of colors and shapes that are visible and ever-changing through the scope. The most fascinating characteristic of a kaleidoscope is that with only a slight turn of the wheel, an entirely new world of shapes and colors appears. It seems almost impossible that the very essence of the shapes and colors remains the same, yet with a simple turn, the picture is remarkably new and different. Likewise, the change picture is still the same, but your slight movement in perspective creates belief in new possibilities, provides vision, restores energy, and gives sense of relief.

We have had the pleasure of watching a few people experience Stage 4 for the first time. It is exciting but unfamiliar territory for them. It might surprise you how many people have never experienced the thrill of "Discovery." Many have only completed the first three stages of the Change Cycle™ and land in The Danger Zone only to continually loop back to Stage 1. There is little wonder why our world is in such turmoil when the basic skills of change are so foreign to so many. Without the desire and basic know-how to implement change on a very personal and practical level, there is very little hope for some people to ever take any significant responsibility for their lives. If individuals were given the opportunity to develop the skills to just get through The Danger Zone to Stage 4, the world would be a better place. The issues of entitlement and "what about me?"

would give way to "I can," "let's do," and a creative "what if?" Our country, our community, and our families would be forever changed for the better.

Please pardon the previous soapbox sermon, but it describes dramatically the importance of Stage 4. The fact is that discovery is a vital part of both the biggest and the tiniest changes you will experience. It becomes your opportunity to begin sculpting the change to be a positive thing in your life. Essentially, Stage 4 invites you to take creative control of the change and your life.

When most people land in Stage 4, they are momentarily stunned because with just a small twist in their actions, they have found themselves with a perspective of wonder, purpose, and possibility. Suddenly, the blinders are pulled away and they can see an array of options and resources that were never obvious before.

The primary experience of Stage 4 is discovery. Most actions are related to the possibility of learning something new, sharing it with others, and exercising your creativity and brainstorming abilities. Another focus is developing relationships with others who "understand" or share the same situation. Stage 4 is where synergy with others is of high value.

A pioneering spirit often emerges, so be aware of your sudden willingness to alter and change other aspects of your life. For example, rearranging the furniture and deciding to redecorate, or cleaning out your closet and deciding it's time for a whole new wardrobe. Take the time to understand Stage 4 because it is the exciting catalyst that provides momentum as you move through the rest of the Change Cycle™.

What Does Stage 4 Look Like?

The children in the four year old class at the Highland Pre-school were making a large gingerbread man cookie. They all took turns adding the ingredients, stirring the cookie dough, and pouring it into the pan. Everybody helped and everybody was very excited.

After they put the gingerbread man in to the oven, they set the timer and went on with their activities. After awhile, the oven timer sounded and all the kids went to check on their cookie. With great anticipation they opened the oven, but the gingerbread man was gone! The children were stunned. Where was he? An observant little one saw the note; the gingerbread man was hiding from them, but he had left them a message. The first clue led them to the second clue and that to the third clue, but still no gingerbread man. The children were beside themselves.

Where had the gingerbread man gone? Suddenly one of the children named Lee called out in an excited voice, "I found him, I found the gingerbread man!" Everyone rushed toward Lee as he pointed, smiling, to the gingerbread man sitting behind the books on the second shelf. The teacher asked Lee how he knew to look there since the clues had led all the other children in a different direction. Lee smiled a proud four year old smile and said, "Because I smelled him, with my nose!"

In Stage 4, you have the opportunity to experience the same kind of discovery process as Lee. Instead of seeing and experiencing only the obvious, you'll have a chance to use all kinds of available resources. Certainly a welcome relief from the occasional trials and tribulations of Stages 1, 2, and 3.

Feelings Of Anticipation

The primary emotional characteristic of Stage 4 is anticipation. Other emotions that branch off of that root are excitement, willingness, and enthusiasm. These emotions are so distinctly different from the emotions of the past three stages, that they have a profound affect on your attitude in an internal and external way. Suddenly, as if by magic, you'll begin to feel that little bit of thrill in the pit of your stomach that makes life exciting. You can never underestimate the power that anticipation can have on your ability to open up to the world of possibilities and new choices.

ANTICIPATION

However, the problem with the experience of anticipation and excitement, is that it can become so easy to enjoy the feelings that you want to ignore the need to use them as a stepping stone for uncovering options.

Thoughts are Creative

Stage 4 is an excellent time to experience your own creativity. Uncovering new ideas, choices, and options is the whole purpose of this stage. Unfortunately, many people fail to notice how creative they really are. However, if you think about it, when most of us think we are pressed to the wall or are under pressure to perform, we can often get really creative. For example, remember the first time as a teenager that you missed your curfew and came in late? You probably came up with some pretty creative reasons to offer your parents! Or, what about the first time you were pulled over by a state trooper for speeding? How many stories ran through your head in a split second that might cause him/her to forgive the infraction? Plenty! That's creativity. Your challenge is to use your ability to "create" when you are not in trouble or under pressure!

If you will allow it, the very nature of Stage 4 will stir your creative juices. The trick is to entertain your ideas, nurture your possibilities, and follow your creations to their conclusion. Some will be usable and viable and others won't, but if you shut creativity down, you are likely to close the door on some of your best options. Take the opportunity to experience yourself as a creative and resourceful person.

Behavior Is Energized

In Stage 3, your mind and body were lethargic and unproductive, so Stage 4 will be a welcome shift. You will notice how much more energy you feel and how much easier it is to be active in your life. When you wake up in the morning, you'll feel rested and ready to go. You'll also find yourself laughing more, participating in your life more, sleeping less, and enjoying interaction with others. All of these advantages come from the energy that is created when we realize there are options and we are in charge of them.

One of the reasons the body and mind feel added energy is the joining of your being with the change. This means rather than fighting with the change, or holding it at arm's distance, you are working with it. This merge is a step to developing a new, more integrated picture of the change.

A trap, however, in Stage 4 is the tendency to want to gather too many new ideas or to associate with and understand every person and their perspective. This can cause the inability to stop, assimilate the facts, and make a decision or take action when necessary. It is important to question yourself in Stage 4 to determine if you are still there because of your need to assimilate and integrate or because you have made it a "comfort zone." In order to move to Stage 5, it is important to gather your options and make a decision about which ones are the best to focus on. Once you've done that, you are ready to move into the final phase of the change.

Since Stage 4 can be fun and interesting; it's easy to want to hang out there. Let's see what *Successful Changers* do to keep moving toward the completion of the Change Cycle™.

Look at the behaviors and language patterns produced by people struggling with the experience of discovery in the following table.

People Who Are Struggling With Discovery	
Behaviors	
• Going around in circles • Following every idea • Overpreparing • Having a false sense of reality • Finding something wrong with all ideas • Wanting to please everyone	
Language Patterns	
• "Someone's going to be hurt unless..." • "I want to pursue all those ideas." • "I am afraid to decide on a solution just yet." • "There my be a better idea out there, so we should wait." • "This option is good, but so are all the others." • "I wonder how I am supposed to decide?"	
Word Descriptions	
• Oppositional • Contented • Hectic	• Overworked • Indecisive • Contradictive

What Do Successful Changers Do?

Successful Changer—Lane Nemeth

Within five minutes, you'll discover that Lane Nemeth is not only reacting to your suggestions, but she's popping with her own, and she's apt to pounce on one of your ideas, give it a quick twist, and come up with something even better. Lane's like that. She's confident, competent, and fun to play with. She's the founder of Discovery Toys.

Lane experienced a dramatic, life-changing experience in 1975. She had a baby. Nothing has been the same since. Lane knew that only the best would do for her daughter, Tara. Like most parents, she had visions of providing her daughter with only the finest toys. This was turning into a win/win of major proportions.

Lane was working for a children's day care center when her daughter was born and was favorably impressed with the center's toys and games. They were unlike the toys she'd seen in the local stores because these toys were designed with the child's long-term needs in mind. They were intended to prompt development and encourage learning. Furthermore, they seemed to be safer and more durable and not one of them was related to war or violence. Lane's curiosity asked, "Why can't parents buy these kinds of toys?"

The answer was disappointing. They were only available to schools through educational materials' suppliers. At the time, developmental toys were seen as "unmarketable" compared with the glitzy, glamorous, shoot-em up, super-whoever celebrity toys, especially when they were being heralded on Saturday morning TV and supported with huge advertising budgets.

"What if," Lane asked herself, "I seek out toys that are instructive, but fun, safe, and durable? I know they are out there and I know other parents want them for their children."

With some money borrowed from her parents and friends, a small nest egg, and the help of a few sympathetic mothers, Lane Nemeth opened Discovery Toys in 1978, working out of the back of her garage in Martinez, California. Since then, she has never looked back. The company is now approaching the $100 million per year sales mark and carries a line of 125 different toys, books, and games distributed by their 30,000 educational consultants around the world.

Lane shares the success of her business by sponsoring Project Self-Esteem, a national award honoring teachers who instill self-worth in their students. Broadening a newly established partnership with the U.S. Committee for UNICEF, Discovery Toys also donates a percentage of select-product proceeds for needy children around the world.

Lane's persistence to discover new ways a child can play has brought smiles to many parents and children alike! Her motto is, "Play is the Pathway to Our Future."

For Lane and other *Successful Changers*, Stage 4 is a very familiar place. They thrive on the energy they create by exploring the possibilities and discovering new options.

People Who Are Successful Acting On Options	
Behaviors	
• Being open to all ideas;never saying no to a possibility	
• Practice seeking perspective	
• Putting greatest strengths to work	
• Taking risks	
• Creating the best solution from all available options	
• Deciding on a plan of action	
Language Patterns	
• "I can see the other points of view better now."	
• "I am ready to take the next step, even if it is risky."	
• "I see my options and I am ready to act."	
• "I am excited about being creative."	
• "It is motivating (exciting) to know that I have choices."	
• "I know whether now is the best time to act."	
Word Descriptions	
• Hopeful	• Optimistic
• Playful	• Available
• Excited	• Active
• Present	• Discerning

There are four skills that *Successful Changers* use to create options and make decisions.

Skill 1: Never Say "No" To An Idea Or Suggestion

Have you ever been in a restaurant and ordered salad instead of french fries only to have the server tell you that "they" don't allow substitutions? When this happens, you know that the *rule* has become more important than the *solution*. By using "they," the server has made it an adversarial issue. Over french fries? Sometimes we have a tendency to do the same by making "the issue" more important than the solution. In Stage 4, there are new options, a sense of discovery, unlimited possibilities. So many people live life by their own strict, private policy and procedure manual that they resist almost instinctively going about anything in a different way. Discover a new way, now!

Allow yourself to be creative. Approach everything in your life as though there were no limitations. If you will do that, you will be amazed at the options that become available. Why not? What have you got to lose? Before long, you will be so excited by the possibilities that present themselves that you will automatically be energized to find a way to make them work!

Though many others had said toys for learning could never compete with the TV toys, Lane said, "Oh, yes they can." She allowed herself to see a need, turn it into a vision, and find a way to make it reality. What if Lane had listened to those who proclaimed "There's no way?" Creativity sees a window where logic sees a wall. Say "yes" first!

Skill 2: Understand And Practice Perspective

In order to identify with change and begin to make it a part of you, it is necessary to see all of the sides. Gaining perspective is a skill that is sometimes difficult, but always worthwhile because it gives you a greater ability to find solutions. Remember that it is easy to have an opinion or a point of view, but it is much more useful to have perspective.

Find a three-year-old and just watch. They are a fine example of perspective because their number-one focus is on discovering the newness in all things. Everyday, three-year-olds live that incredible sense of discovery that most of us have lost as grown-ups.

If for twelve minutes we could be as curious as a three-year-old, willing to check out all the "neat stuff" around us, our perspective would broaden to include things we've never dreamed of. This is a good time to reacquaint yourself with the playful child inside you! (You know he/she is there because you experienced the naughty side of your three-year-old self in Stage 2!)

Perspective also serves to help us make better decisions because we approach ideas with multi-dimensional information and thinking. If you see an idea or option from only one point-of-view, you are missing the point. Perspective gives choices.

In Lane's story, it is clear that she had the perspective of her idea through the eyes of a child, a teacher, a mother, and a businesswoman. This perspective was part of what convinced her that this new business venture was an idea whose time had come. We can hardly help but reiterate that Lane's company was appropriately named Discovery Toys!

Skill 3: Identify And Use Your Strengths

The problem for most of us is that we deny our strengths by always talking about and affirming our weaknesses. Stop that now! You have strengths that are a vital and daily part of your personality. They are part of the survival skills that are built into every human being.

One of the benefits of being around *Successful Changers* is that they are happy to contribute their skills and strengths to others. They are very clear about what they have to offer and do so gladly. Many people spend a lot of time berating themselves to the point of believing that they really have very little to contribute. The good news is that everyone has strengths to offer. It's a simple matter of knowing or, in some cases, admitting what those strengths are. Ultimately, if we fail to accentuate and use our strengths, we will be left to battle with our weaknesses. If you will infuse your strengths into your ideas, you can create incredible results for yourself.

If Lane had focused on her weaknesses (i.e., no business training, no knowledge about toys, no money), she would surely have walked away from her idea. Instead, Lane accentuated her strengths (love of children, love of learning, determination, focus) and used them to overcome her weaknesses. That resource is available within all of us!

Skill 4: Be Willing To Take Risks!

Mention the idea of taking risks and many people see drastic pictures like skydiving or bungee jumping. Maybe you picture things like starting your own business, getting married, or investing in the stock market as situations that are "risky." At any rate, most people shy away from anything other than "playing it safe."

Interestingly enough, *Successful Changers* are moderate risk-takers. For them, it is simply a matter of taking one step at a time. No leaps, no jumping off cliffs, just the willingness to put one foot in front of the other and continue moving forward.

Imagine yourself driving at night in very dense fog. When you look out through the windshield, you can only see the road as far as the dim lights will shine; maybe ten feet. You have no idea what's coming toward you or what lies ahead, but you do know that little-by-little, you can see ahead and that is progress.

That's the sort of risk that successful change requires. You must learn to put one foot forward into the fog, knowing that once you do, there will be additional information for the next step.

For example, a woman named Sandy knows that her job is going to be phased out within the next three months. She may be laid off or trained for another job.

As a risky step, Sandy looks around and notes the jobs in the company she might enjoy. Then, she goes and sells her skills and talents to the appropriate manager. Doesn't that seem simple? Unfortunately, most people sit and wait for fate to take its course. Learn to take the very next step, it may be that step from the fog into the sunshine.

What risks did Lane from Discovery Toys take? She borrowed money, she did what other people said wouldn't work, and she entered a global market to find the kind of toys she was looking for. It's a good thing she was willing to take one step after another. Those steps have added up to one success after another for Lane Nemeth and the people of Discovery Toys!

Now that you are ready to leave the yellow stages, notice how being stuck in them can bring distractions that delay progress or they can provide motivation that provides forward momentum. Use the momentum you have created to move on to Stage 5! If you'll work with these skills, you'll find that a lot of areas of your life will improve.

Stage 4 Skills Building

1. *For one day, take the morning and be aware of how many times you have the tendency to say "no" to an idea, a new way of doing something or a different option, etc. Take the afternoon to shift your perspective and see how easy it is to say "yes" or "maybe" first!*

2. *Find a child under six years old and ask them these three questions:*

   How big is a swimming pool?

   How big is a lake?

   How big is the ocean?

3. *Notice their perspective. What thoughts and/or feelings did you notice within yourself?*

4. *Name something you'd like to do that would involve a risk. What would be the very first step? How easy would it be for you to take it?*

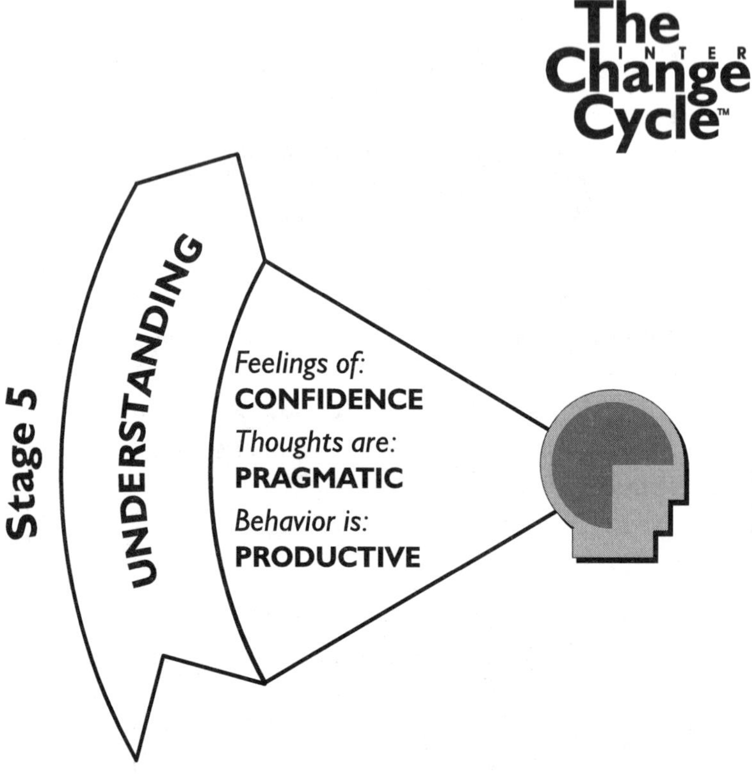

Stage 5—The Change Becoming Me	
Primary Experience:	**Understanding**
Major Focus:	**Accomplishment**
Stage Objective:	**Knowing the benefits of the change**
Motivated By:	**Features or benefits**
Overuses:	**Pride**
Challenge:	**Keep moving to complete the Change Cycle™**
Opportunity:	**Acknowledging assistance and support from others**

"Some luck lies in not getting what you thought you wanted, but getting what you have, which, once you have it, you may be smart enough to see is what you would have wanted had you known."

Garrison Keillor

Chapter 9

The Change Becoming Me

Stage 5: Understanding

Entering the green stages finally brings you to the place of deliberately moving with the change. While the red stages helped you deal with what "was" and the yellow stages helped assimilate what was "ahead," the green stages encourage you to step into the change and embrace it as your own. Now is the time to move through the final stages of the change process. The green Stages are certainly easier to move through, but they still have an up and down side that calls for some respect or you can still get stuck.

In Stage 5, our primary experience is one of understanding. After this change journey of frequent confusion and indecision, it is a treat to have the lights come on to illuminate why this change has been important.

As people travel through the early stages of the change process, they're often heard to say, "I don't understand why this is happening, but I have to trust that everything happens for a reason." Well, Stage 5 reveals the reason! Whatever the purpose, whatever good has come, whatever lessons have been learned, all come to light in a new way in Stage 5. The peace that comes with understanding can make it easy to convince yourself that you are finished with the change. This is a very dangerous assumption because it may cause you to stop short of successfully completing the Change Cycle™. Keep in mind that understanding something doesn't necessarily mean that it has integrated itself into your life.

It may well be that this stage is the trickiest of all. Remember the last time you watched a child with a new toy? Surely, the child ignored all his/her old toys and gave total attention to the new one. However, there came a time when the toy was no longer new and the child discarded it and put attention elsewhere.

Metaphorically, we can experience the same thing. Our new sense of understanding can be like a new toy. We enjoy the awareness and the change becomes something to which we gladly give our attention. But if we only "play" with our understanding, we may find that the change is also soon discarded and our attention put elsewhere before the work is completed. Stay with Stage 5 because you still have a short way to go, and it's worth it.

What Does Stage 5 Look Like?

When my plane reached the appropriate altitude, the flight attendant announced that dinner would soon be served. Generally that news is about as satisfying as turbulence, but I was in for a very pleasant surprise. Julie, the flight attendant, asked me if I'd like penne pasta with gouda cheese or smoked chicken salad. I was stunned since all I had expected was rubber chicken or peanuts. I chose the pasta and believe it or not, it was excellent. What a treat! And yet, getting a good pasta dish is not generally considered big news. It does say a lot about the expectations of plane food.

I later asked the flight attendant what was going on with the food changes on Northwest Airlines. She smiled and began to tell me how the Airline had surveyed its customers and the overwhelming service request was for better in-flight food. The Airline's executives decided to go all out to respond to the customers' request. They hired chefs from different regions of the country and put them in charge to create an entirely new approach to airline food. Though it was a huge risk and a big challenge, new menus and vendors were selected, and the experiment was underway.

I asked Julie what she thought about the change and she admitted that she had originally been skeptical, but was pleasantly surprised at the new ideas the team of chefs had come up with. However, even with the exiting new food, she was concerned that cynical travelers would laugh it off as another gimmick. She smiled and said her fears were unfounded because many people had said the food tasted great and she had even had a few people ask for second helpings. She admitted that people were actually thanking her for the meal and seemed to be in a better mood throughout the flight. Julie made it clear that the benefits had certainly made the project worthwhile.

This is a typical experience in Stage 5. Julie and her co-workers doubted the project would go anywhere. Making the changes caused them to have to alter their routine. Even though the ideas seemed good, putting them into "real life" seemed an unlikely prospect. These are all issues you have experienced through the change process. Stage 5 will make clear the benefits that this change has created for you.

Feelings Of Confidence

As understanding increases, so does confidence, the kind of confidence that acknowledges a job well done and builds self-esteem. As you experience this confidence, you will find that it also has a humbling quality to it that includes gratitude to those who have helped you, as well as appreciation for your perseverance.

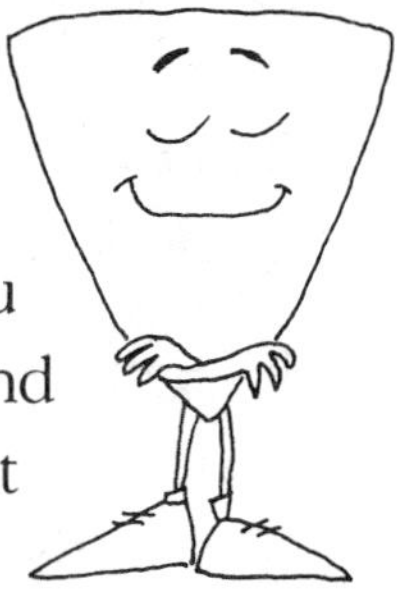

CONFIDENCE

When Stage 5 is experienced to the fullest, it allows you to know the kind of confidence that is healthy and resourceful.

The resourcefulness of this confidence is primarily manifested in your willingness to take decisive action related to the change. It is as though you have sure footing and a firm foundation, where before the ground beneath you seemed a bit shaky. This makes Stage 5 an excellent time to get a lot accomplished.

Thoughts Are Pragmatic

To be pragmatic simply means to be practical. So, in Stage 5, your thinking becomes much more infused with common sense. You'll find yourself better able to conceptualize what is happening and, therefore, apply it to your everyday life more easily. This also means that your thinking becomes more flexible and it is easier to see the many dimensions of the change. Once that happens, your thinking and subsequent actions become much more deliberate. As you enjoy the ability to see things more practically, beware of the tendency you might have to think that you have mastered the change. Stay with it so that you can move on to the final Stage.

Behavior Is Productive

Fortunately, Stage 5 allows us to more than make up in productivity whatever was lost in Stage 3.

People are frequently amazed at how much they get done once they reach Stage 5. Of course, this tends to build self-esteem, which in turn gives the body and mind added energy. This usually means an extra dose of enthusiasm is also present. Since enthusiasm can sometimes mask the results, make sure that your productive efforts are producing the results you want and need.

Once you recognize the signs of Stage 5, keep in mind that your primary objective is to identify the benefits of this change. Ultimately, you have to find your own personal benefit in something or you'll discard it. Conversely, once you identify your benefits, you become more and more invested in the change. It becomes more a part of you.

Sadly, some people never make it this far in the Change Cycle™, so they rarely get to experience this good feeling. Now that you know "how" to get here, let's look at some of the skills you can practice in order to experience Stage 5 often and to the fullest.

Look at the behaviors and language patterns of people struggling with understanding in the following table.

People Who Are Struggling With Understanding	
Behaviors	
• Becoming insensitive • Being very structured, rigid or rule-oriented • Being domineering or dictatorial • Overpreparing • Confused/Contradicting	
Language Patterns	
• "I have to do this now." • "I'm tired of everyone dragging their feet." • "I'll decide, alone." • "This is the way I'm going to do it." • "I don't care if others don't understand what's going on."	
Word Descriptions	
• Conceited • Naive • Discourteous • Bull-headed • Intolerant	• Insensitive • Heartless • Petty • Inconsistent

What Do Successful Changers Do?

Successful Changer—Jinger Heath

The following story gives insight into what *Successful Changers* do in order to understand the benefits of the change.

Jinger and Richard Heath bought a floundering cosmetics company in 1981, infused it with their energy and vitality, and changed it forever. This company is BeautiControl Cosmetics of Carrollton, Texas. The Heaths put everything on the line to make their dream of owning their own business come true and that dream paid off. Jinger Heath and BeautiControl were recently named by the National Foundation for Women Business Owners and *Working Women* magazine to the list of Top Fifty Women Owned Businesses in the United States and has repeatedly been recognized as one of the fastest growing and best managed companies in America by both *Forbes* and *Business Week*.

Juggling the responsibilities of her growing company and the responsibilities of her children and family, Jinger was a busy woman. As if that wasn't enough, she found two lumps in her breast. The fear of cancer became very real, very quickly. Now she had to face the potential change cancer could make in her life. Jinger was blessed with the news that her cysts were benign. For a woman who had built her career on encouraging other women to look their best and to have a positive attitude in all situations, her experience gave her a fresh new perspective.

One of the most heart fulfilling projects for Jinger was producing a comprehensive "how-to" guide to looking and feeling good for women undergoing chemotherapy or suffering from other conditions that might affect their physical appearance. Entitled, *Well Beauty: A New Beginning*, the booklet is designed to help women look their best and keep a positive attitude. "Writing *Well Beauty* was a natural progression of everything I've learned about the effects of positive thinking and looking your best can have on your recovery." said Ms. Heath.

BeautiControl's commitment to women goes beyond offering top-of-the-line products and unique career opportunities. "We believe that a woman's overall self-assurance and her success is affected by the strength and impact of her total image." states Jinger. "When a woman knows what makes her look and feel her best, she builds confidence in herself. That confidence has changed the lives of thousands of women, mine included!"

Jinger's belief in and passion for caring about the "whole woman," motivated her to establish W.H.O. (Women Helping Others), a non-profit foundation dedicated to encouraging and recognizing the humanitarian effort of women for women. "Through W.H.O., we are giving back to our community by focusing on issues that are important to women. With the activities created by the Foundation, I hope to reach people in need and give them a chance for a better tomorrow." The W.H.O. Foundation operates with no administrative costs or expenses because of the generous contribution of staff and resources by BeautiControl. "We are proud to be able to say that the donations that come into the W.H.O. Foundation go directly towards reaching women," Jinger said.

The objectives of the Foundation include supporting and contributing to both national and local charities and through their awards program honoring women for special service in their communities. They will also continue to develop literature and videos on beauty and "total image" advice for women facing health challenges, as well as engage in activities, programs, and services related to supporting, encouraging, and recognizing the efforts of women for women.

"I know that one person can make a difference. I know that with passion you can change anything," Jinger said with a sense of determined confidence. She would know.

Review the following table. It shows the behavior and language patterns *Successful Changers* use to help themselves see the benefits of change.

People Who Are Successful Seeing Benefits	
Behaviors	
• Being inclusive • Listening to and being open to suggestions • Being fair • Showing appreciation • Being even tempered • Celebrating victories • Focusing on benefits	
Language Patterns	
• "I know what I need to do and I'm ready to do it." • "I feel good about this." • "I'm moving forward." • "I'm glad that other people have stuck with me." • "I understand what this change is really all about."	
Word Descriptions	
• Caring • Balanced • Open-minded • Patient	• Centered • Pleased • Decisive • Approachable

In Stage 5 there are three basic skills that *Successful Changers* utilize to understand the change and reap its benefits.

Skill 1: Identify The Benefits

In Stage 5, your thoughts will automatically steer you toward consideration of the benefits in the change. Notice, however, that in order to move to Stage 6, the benefits must be clear and defined. There will always be plenty of people around to remind you of the potential problems, so it's important to be acutely aware of the benefits. Remember too that little benefits can be just as important as big ones.

A common mistake in identifying benefits is confusing them with features. Understanding the difference between features and benefits will aid you in monitoring what is motivating you, as well as assist you in staying focused. In simple terms:

Features = external advantages

Benefits = internal advantages.

For example, if you've been on a diet and have progressed to Stage 5, the features might be: a new wardrobe, compliments on how you look, and reaching your ideal weight. The benefits might be higher self-esteem, better health, more confidence, and increased personal pride.

It is important to note that, with time, the features go away. The new clothes are no longer new and people stop complimenting you because they get used to your new size. That's the reason it is so important to specifically name the benefits.

Having had a brush with the prospect of breast cancer, Jinger understood that the benefit of her experience was a new awareness of how much a disease can alter your image of yourself. Suddenly, the features of physical beauty paled in comparison to the benefits of looking good as a way of building confidence and optimism. Suddenly, Jinger's business took on a depth of meaning that might never have been realized without her personal change experience.

Skill 2: Give Credit Where Credit Is Due

When you're feeling energized and productive and you have a new freedom from all the pressure, take time to remember those who have helped you get there. It's important to be aware that you are often so busy "just surviving" that you forget about the ones who are being supportive. Take time, celebrate, and be grateful to God, your friends and family, and to yourself.

Successful Changers know that they rarely get this far without the help and support of at least one other person. However, they also go a step further. *Successful Changers* realize how important it is to acknowledge those who have helped and supported them. Sometimes this means privately saying "thank you" in some kind way and sometimes it means giving credit where credit is due in public. The important thing is to take the time to give appreciation to others.

During an awards banquet for the National Meeting of Citizens Against Crime, Edna Harrell of New Orleans, Louisiana, was honored as one of the top program marketers in the country. As she made her way to the stage, everyone jumped to their feet and began to applaud and cheer. You see, Edna was eighty years old, she had a mentally retarded son who lived with her, and she had to ride the bus for one hour (and two transfers) every day to get to work! As Edna received the award, it would have been easy for her to accent her accomplishments in the face of incredible odds but, when Edna began to speak, she acknowledged and thanked her Regional Director and the other staff in her office. She made it perfectly clear that she was a member of a team and they were a significant part of her success. Edna knows how to give credit where credit is due.

Acknowledgement is powerful. It is a profound reminder that we need other people and so rarely do we accomplish anything alone.

Jinger will be the first to tell you that the accomplishments of the WHO Foundation are due primarily to the women who have bravely fought against life-threatening illnesses. Jinger knows that her actions are a response to their courage and they, too, deserve the credit.

Skill 3: Celebrate Your Progress

In some of our public seminars, we do what's called a "Board Break." Yes, that means all the participants break a one inch thick pine board in half with their bare hands! As you might imagine, there is often fear and hesitation at the thought of doing such a thing. As we go through the process of preparing everyone, we have participants practice everything they need to do in order to safely break the board. That practice includes celebrating! We've noticed that celebration seems to be a difficult thing for some people to practice. However, after someone breaks their board, there is instant celebration—spontaneous, unbridled celebration! In fact, everyone in the room celebrates as each board is broken! People can hardly believe they have done such a thing. The energy and momentum created by the "breakthrough" is phenomenal.

Be sure, when you get to Stage 5, there will be reason to celebrate and even brag! *Successful Changers* believe it and do it. They know that celebration is necessary to positively *anchor* the change experience. By positive anchoring, we mean associating an accomplishment with a physical celebration. By doing so, when a similar achievement is repeated, the positive memory of the first accomplishment and its celebration will again be present. Celebration also keeps the attention on all you've gained through the change process.

There are many ways to celebrate. When the participants in our seminars celebrate breaking their boards, they do everything from a silent pumping of their fist to jumping up and down and screaming YES! We all have different ways of celebrating successes and that's great. You know, just do it!

In her own way, Jinger has created an avenue for women to celebrate in the face of illness and even death. As she puts it, "Every day is a chance for them to celebrate life by feeling good about themselves."

Stay with it! There is only one more stage to go, and it is an important one. Use the energy created by your confidence to take you through your last step—Stage 6!

These three skills are the keys to navigating through of Stage 5. If you stay focused on progressing to Stage 6, you will experience incredible personal and/or professional growth. Otherwise, you will stagnate and lose momentum. Commit yourself to action!

Stage 5 Skills Building

1. *List three features and three benefits of the change you are experiencing. Which ones surprised you? Why did they?*

2. *Think of a time when someone acknowledged you as part of their success. How did you feel? When was the last time you acknowledged or thanked someone? When will be the next time?*

3. *List five ways you can celebrate your progress. Act on at least one of them.*

The InterChange Cycle™

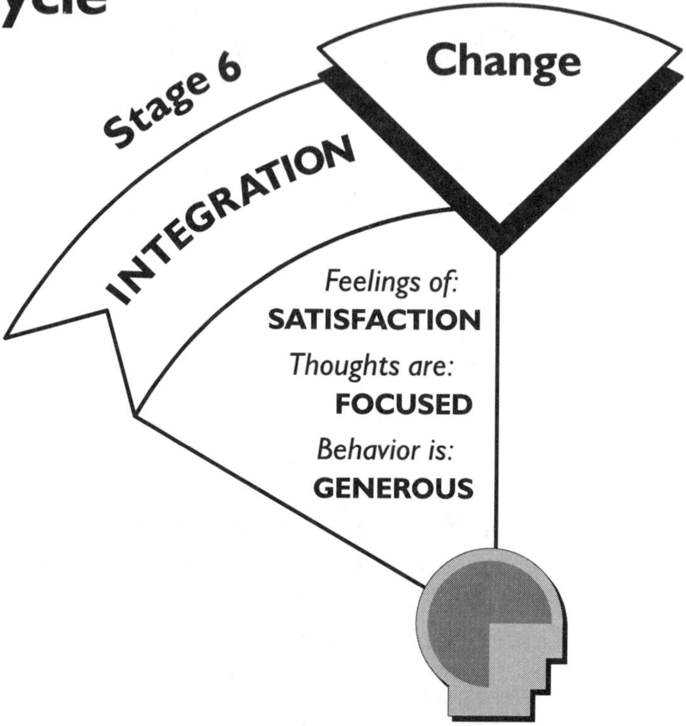

Stage 6—I Am The Change	
Primary Experience:	**Integration**
Major Focus:	**Learning new skills**
Stage Objective:	**Stability**
Motivated By:	**Recognition or ego**
Overuses:	**Arrogance**
Challenge:	**Avoid becoming complacent**
Opportunity:	**Successfully make the change a part of your life**

"Strangely enough, this is the past someone in the future is longing to go back to."

Ashleigh Brilliant

Chapter 10

I Am The Change

Stage 6: Integration

The title of this Chapter, "I Am The Change," tells the whole story about this Stage. The entire purpose of this final step is to internalize the change so completely that it becomes a part of who you are. Without Stage 6, we would put ourselves at tremendous risk of discarding the change much like a child discards a toy after the newness wears off. For this reason, it is important to integrate the change into your life. Think of a jigsaw puzzle that is put together except for three or four pieces. The one thing that stands out about the puzzle is the missing pieces. Now you can get an idea of what change without integration looks like. The missing pieces become the focus rather than the whole picture. Once the three or four pieces are in their place, the puzzle becomes an integrated picture.

The major focus for Stage 6 is to put the final pieces together so that the change holds together and a complete picture is created.

Remember the sound of a Tupperware™ lid when it locks into place? In Stage 6, you "lock in" the change so that it becomes more normal than alien. Integration happens much like that as you learn to maintain a pattern of consistency that makes the change a part of your life. When you get to Stage 6, chances are you'll find that the change is now familiar, yet you still have a ways to go before it will be like brushing your teeth.

In Stage 6 you can hardly help but to like yourself. Inside, you can feel yourself being congruent and balanced in your thoughts, feelings, and actions. That is a powerful place to be. Your congruence or stability will attract others to you, while you will be attracted to those who can teach you.

The challenge of Stage 6 is arrogance. Being "full of yourself" is a sure path to loneliness. Arrogance is a mask of fear caused by a person trying to make accomplishments of the past be excuses for the future. Such a narrow perspective focuses all the attention on yourself and pushes the change away instead of embracing and integrating it. By keeping sight of the big picture, the little issues stay little, helping to keep you focus on the change.

The critical part of Stage 6 is realizing how important it is to finish the Change Cycle™. Remember that completing the Change Cycle™ is how you begin to clean out and replace the faulty ways of thinking that developed in your brain before you had an adequate "change map." Every time you successfully complete the Change Cycle™, you add a positive and resourceful example of change to your memory, so it can support you better in the future. Conversely, if you never finish a change, you are risking adding more experiences to your memory that are rooted in Stages 1, 2, and 3. Imagine what it would be like to step into a new change knowing the consistent success of reaching Stage 6. This is an opportunity for your schema to be forever changed.

What Does Stage 6 Look Like?

Ten years ago, almost everyone knew "Famous Amos," the smiling chocolate chip cookie giant. Having started with his grandmother's recipe and a big dream, Wally Amos built his cookie business into an $80 million success. But in the mid-1980s, Amos faced a cash flow crunch that put him in jeopardy of losing everything. It was hard to believe that in the midst of his greatest visibility and success, Wally Amos' company could be faced with such turmoil. His cookies were so popular and his name so respected. Before long, investors took over Amos' company, pushing him out, and even stripping him of the rights to use his own name. Wally Amos had lost almost everything he had.

Yet Amos never lost his determination. The tough times were tough, but as he pulled himself up, he began to focus on what he could do in the midst of these challenges. Wally Amos knows cookies. The cookie business had brought him his greatest successes and his greatest failures. He knew he had to try again. That realization was the birth of a new venture called "The Uncle No-name Cookie Company". Wally began to sell himself again and his cookies. Several major chains gladly carry his new products today.

Perhaps the most fascinating thing about Amos is his contagious happiness. No matter what it is, he has the ability to learn the lessons that life presents to him. In retrospect, Amos knows that he acted out of fear and didn't pay close enough attention to the management of his company. Wally Amos boldly pronounces that he never allows himself to be a victim. He does this by taking responsibility for the circumstances of his life, past and present, by learning from them, and when appropriate, changing them. With this story in mind, learn about the feelings, thoughts, and behaviors of Stage 6.

Feelings Of Satisfaction

The picture of satisfaction that comes to mind is one of relaxing and putting your feet up after an outstanding meal. Ultimate food satisfaction comes from eating just the right amount. Too much can be miserable and too little can be frustrating. With this concept in mind,

think about Stage 6 as a place of balance. There's nothing quite like the contentment of knowing that all is well.

Of course, there is an inherent danger in becoming so satisfied and content. We lull our way into thinking that nothing can spoil or intrude on our way of life. Beware! The place of satisfaction should be used as a support to anticipate the future, not as an excuse to become arrogant, stubborn, or stagnant.

Thoughts Are Focused

After the rather scattered, searching experiences of the other stages in the Change Cycle™, the ability to focus is a welcome relief! This experience will offer you the opportunity to be productive and add clarity to all you do in your life.

Imagine for a minute the power of a laser compared to the power of a light bulb. Stage 6 actually gives you a chance to have laser focus rather than scattered light. Perhaps this is one of the great advantages of successfully completing the Change Cycle™. It gives you the ability to effectively apply yourself through your ability to focus. All too often we choose to let change distract us and, therefore, render us ineffective. For all of you who may want to argue for things to stay the same, remember that things will change no matter what you decide and, consequently, you'll be thrown into a state of instability and chaos.

With the ability to focus on the issues that you have deemed most important, you will see your management of time improve, your contributions to your family increase, and your energy level skyrocket. You will also find it much easier to look at the future and focus on what you want next in your life!

Behavior Is Generous

The word, "generous" may puzzle you a bit, but it truly is descriptive of the behavior we see in Stage 6. Generosity, in this case, indicates the almost spontaneous willingness to give something back. It's almost as if you notice the opportunities to give that before, might have eluded you. Suddenly, you find yourself offering to be of help to others who may be struggling with a change similar to one you've been through.

When people become part of important social causes (i.e., AIDS, civil rights, victim's rights, fund raising), it usually stems from the successful completion of a change that was somehow related to that cause. Likewise, people often make new career decisions as a result of getting to Stage 6 during an important change in their life. This happens because of the profound need to offer something to others that may assist them as they face their own important life changes. Obviously, these big manifestations of generosity are very noticeable, but the behavior exists in little ways as well. For example, at work people offer to help co-workers. At home, a family member does something nice for another. In the community, a person volunteers in an organization that meets a particular need. All of this stems from the need and desire to give back.

It behooves us all to consider what a better world this would be if more people experienced Stage 6 more of the time. It stands to reason that many of our societal ills would disappear because we would work toward consensus, reconciliation and win-win outcomes.

Look at the behaviors and language patterns of people who struggle with integrating the change into their lives.

People Who Are Struggling With Integration	
Behaviors	
• Failing to be responsive to their environment or reacting to their environment • Wanting to do things their own way • Giving themselves credit for everything good that happens • Often pointing to their own accomplishments and other's failures • Making change a part of their ego	
Language Patterns	
• "If it ain't broke, don't fix it." • "It's my way or the highway." • "I'm the one others should learn from." • "If I'm able to do this, then anyone can."	
Word Descriptions	
• Boastful • Self-serving • Cocky • Pretentious	• Narrow • Vain • Delusional • Arrogant

What Do Successful Changers Do?

Successful Changer—Boomer Esiason

Sometimes when you give, it is because you can. Sometimes it's because you want to. And sometimes it's because you have to. You have to give in, give up and put it all on the line.

Boomer was used to sharing. From his childhood through his adult years he loved the fun and frenzy of being surrounded by lots of people; family, friends and teammates. He thrived when everybody was watching and in New York he had become quite the show. He kept the crowds cheering on the weekends and the kids smiling during the week. Boomer always seemed to have time for a quick visit to a children's hospital, or time to help raise money for one charity or another.

This guy, with the heart-warming smile, the body of a Viking and the gentle spirit of a teddy bear could claim the same amount of energy as a three-ring circus. Boomer is an appropriate nickname for this man who lives life in a "large" fashion. He is, in some ways, easy to describe; caring and supportive of his community, a leader, a winner, and his greatest joy, a father.

Gunnar's birth was a blessing that only a parent can understand. Boomer and Cheryl poured out their love to their beautiful baby boy. But Gunnar was having a tough time. He was often sick and the doctors could not identify the cause. His little body was taking longer to recover with each new illness, and his pain and suffering were torturing his parents.

Gunnar's dad is big, tall, and quick. He needs to be because his job is to avoid even bigger men from running him down and throwing him on the ground, as hard as they can—that's called a tackle. Certainly pain must be its synonym. As an NFL quarterback, you are supposed to be fearless and tough, and at all costs, avoid tackling or being tackled.

But fearless and tough are useless when your little boy is sick and hurting and you don't know why. Boomer Esiason, former pro-bowl quarterback and star of the New York Jets, was scared; scared of his two-year-old son's condition, scared of not knowing what the cause was and afraid to find out.

The doctors finally determined that Gunnar had cystic fibrosis. Boomer's heart ached because of his comparison of his vibrant health compared to his little boy's fragile body. In order to be there for Gunnar, to help him fight the disease, Boomer considered quitting football.

Boomer prayed that he might utilize his strength for his sick child. His prayers were soon answered. He realized that standing with Gunnar could only help so much, yet standing up for him was a special gift few could give. Boomer knew that a cure for the disease was close, only time and money away. He dedicated his football career, his energy, his love and his life to claiming victory over cystic fibrosis for Gunnar and all the children it affected.

Boomer was sure that if he and the Jets had a successful season, people would listen and respond to anything he had to say. He was right. He told Gunnar's story every chance he had. They appeared together on television, at fund raisers, in magazines and newspapers all over the country. The message about cystic fibrosis was reaching people and they were taking action. They are giving their time, their money and their prayers for a little boy and his dad, and for all those fighting the disease.

Boomer Esiason will never be completely satisfied until cystic fibrosis has a cure. Be clear though, this great NFL quarterback has scored his greatest victory, not with a touchdown pass, but by tackling a life-threatening disease.

Take a look at the following table. It shows the behavior and language patterns of*Successful Changers* like Boomer use to help themselves succeed in finding stability.

People Who Are Successful Creating Stability	
Behaviors	
• Taking advantage of growth opportunities • Offering assistance to others • Being open to what the future holds • Having appropriate, adult responses • Making change a part of their growth	
Language Patterns	
• "I have grown a lot through this experience." • "I am happy with how this has turned out/affected me." • "I feel confident about my ability to adjust." • "I can make this work."	
Word Descriptions	
• Powerful • Competent • Peaceful • Confident • Progressive	• Responsible • Expansive • Expectant • Eager

Skill 1: Gain New Knowledge

Part of gaining new knowledge is looking toward the future. Consider gaining some new knowledge that would be useful to you as you stabilize within the change. It may be a new skill or an advanced class in an area you already know. Maybe you could enroll in a seminar or retreat as an opportunity to further your self-image or money management. Whatever the case, keep learning and growing.

It is important to remember that in this stage, you are in an emotional and mental place that will enhance learning. Take advantage of the time when your mind is eager and open.

Another part of gaining new knowledge is allowing the past to be a teacher. In other words, take an inventory of the change process you've been through and gain as much understanding about yourself as possible. Ask yourself what you've learned, where you faltered, and where you showed strength!

If you look carefully at Boomer's story, you will find the consistent commitment he has had to learn about living with cystic fibrosis. Once Boomer completed the Change Cycle™ around his son's illness, he began to educate others.

Skill 2: Offer Assistance To Others

The generosity that comes with this stage can be channeled to help others who might not be as far along in the Change Cycle™ process. Sometimes this assistance takes the form of emerging leadership qualities. Sometimes it takes the form of giving back to your community, church or someone else struggling with change.

As you stabilize with your change, that is, as it becomes more of a normal part of you, consider how you might help others. This is your chance to share your leadership qualities. People sometimes tell us that they have a difficult time seeing themselves as a leader. They think of leaders as presidents of nations, owners of companies, heads of religious organizations, spokespersons for great causes, etc. It is true that all these people are in leadership positions. However, it is also true that every person has the ability to be a leader in some way. If nothing else, you have led yourself through this change and now you're in Stage 6.

There are as many definitions of leadership as there are stars in the sky. The important point to remember is that whatever leadership means to you, and whatever qualities and characteristics you value in another person or in yourself, these are the values for you to model and share. Whether you affect the whole world or just one other person, your leadership has made a difference.

Skill 3: Be Flexible

Another important value of *Successful Changers* is "flexibility." We have a tendency to think of change in the context of the relatively big events that enter our lives and alter everything familiar. We may also jump to the conclusion that mastering the big changes makes us flexible. While it's certainly fair to say that you will have become more adaptable, it may not mean that you have mastered the art of flexibility.

Flexibility is a form of fine-tuning and it is, at times, both an art and a science. Flexibility is the resilience we show when little things disrupt our lives and alter what we were expecting. Little things like:

- The boss is late for a meeting.
- A fender-bender slows traffic significantly.
- Your plane is an hour late.
- Rain interferes with your exercise regimen.
- You win $2.7 million in the lottery.
- Old friends are traveling through your city and drop in unexpectedly.
- Your husband/wife is late for dinner and it is ruined.
- Your child gets the flu.
- Your co-worker cancels lunch at the last minute after insisting that it was important that you get together.
- Your luggage is lost at the airport.

You get the picture. There are dozens of these everyday occurrences and for most of us, these are the things that create incredible stress. Your challenge is to recognize them and quickly take steps to get back on track.

If we go to nature for flexibility models, we need only watch the trees when the wind is blowing. The limbs sway back and forth, moving easily with the breeze. If a tree resisted and attempted to remain upright and stiff (like the brittle, rigid wood of a dead tree), it would break against the pressure of the wind. By being pliable and movable, the living tree is able to remain standing.

Successful Changers use motivational self-talk as opposed to the self-talk most other people use.

Flexibility Self-Talk	
Struggling With Change	**Successful With Change**
▪ "What problems does this create for me?"	• "How can I make this work?
▪ "How does this take advantage of me?"	• "What is the advantage in this?"
▪ "This probably means...." (assume bad)	• "This might mean..." (assume good)
▪ "How do I feel about this now?"	• "How will I feel about this next week?"
▪ I should react to this immediately."	• "I'll gather more information before responding."
▪ "*They* are responsible for ruining my day."	• "I can be responsible for what to do now."

As you can see, the self-talk of those struggling with change is a downward spiral that creates tremendous resistance and stress. Conversely, the self-talk of those successful with change propels them to find solutions and actions which release stress.

It should be noted that flexibility comes in many disguises, so we must beware. There are people who meekly say okay to whatever comes along and appear to be flexing amiably. However, inside they are engaging in the self-talk of a victim. Such self-talk takes a terrible toll on their emotions and bodies. Other people accept the interruptions, smile, and work around them, but when they get the chance, blow up because they feel used and mistreated. Still others, appear to be flexible about some things and not others. This probably indicates that issues which have little impact on them get a flexible response, while issues that are important to them get a more apprehensive response. All of these examples simply disguise resistance! Sooner or later, as the prophets of old have said, "What doesn't bend will break". What we want to learn from *Successful Changers* is this:

> *Flexibility means to consistently bend and flow for the purpose of creating resolution and forward movement.*

Now that you have mastered Stage 6, remember to anticipate the changes that are in your future! You are ready to handle them because you have learned a secret of change, understanding the Change Cycle™.

Once again, we have to acknowledge that the significant difference between *Successful Changers* and others is that they use these simple skills.

Stage 6 Skills Building

1. ***In what areas would added knowledge or personal growth be most useful to you? What specific skills or knowledge are you seeking?***

2. ***Recall a time when you assisted someone else through a rough situation or showed them how to do a hard task. What help or assistance can you offer someone now as a result of this change?***

"It is not the strongest of the species that survives, nor the most intelligent, but rather the one most responsive to change."

Charles Darwin

Chapter 11

Change: Building Bridges to Your Future

It stands to reason that the more we understand this thing called change, the better equipped we are to manage with it effectively and successfully. By understanding the six Stages of your response to change, you have opened the door to new awareness and new possibilities. As you model what *Successful Changers* believe and do, you will open yourself to a whole universe of satisfying change experiences. Just those two things, believing and doing will make a big difference in your life.

Some of you will want to go to an even deeper level of understanding; a level which gives you the opportunity to flow easily and effectively with life. This Chapter simply reflects the truths that *Successful Changers* have learned by working effectively with change over and over again.

Successful Changers know at a very personal level that their responsiveness and ability to change quickly and effectively, gives them an edge and a freedom that few others possess.

There are four response—abilities *Successful Changers* use. Three of them you've been exposed to already. The fourth is about unresourceful patterns that you might find yourself in and how *Successful Changers* handle them.

Response—Abilities of Successful Changers
1. I understand the six Stages of my personal response to change, how I respond generally and my specific response tendencies in change situations.
2. I consistently practice and use the skills that create my successful change attitudes and beliefs.
3. I know that "being flexible" always gives me new options and enables me to use perspective to my advantage.
4. I am alert and aware when unresourceful patterns emerge and I stop them immediately.

As you go through the Change Cycle™, developing your awareness of the unresourceful patterns that can surface and trap you will save you time and potential pain or frustration. As you consistently notice and experience the six Stages, you will identify your own change pattern tendencies. But there are three general patterns or traps to watch out for.

Recognizing The Traps

Pattern 1: Being Stuck In A Stage

There is always a consequence if you defy the cyclical nature of change. If you become stagnant by remaining in a particular stage, you begin to work against the process. This is one of the easiest problems to identify because you only need to recognize that you are repeating feelings, behaviors, and thoughts over and over and over again. However, it can be the most difficult to overcome because repetition, fueled by fear or lack of motivation, creates incredible intensity and inertia.

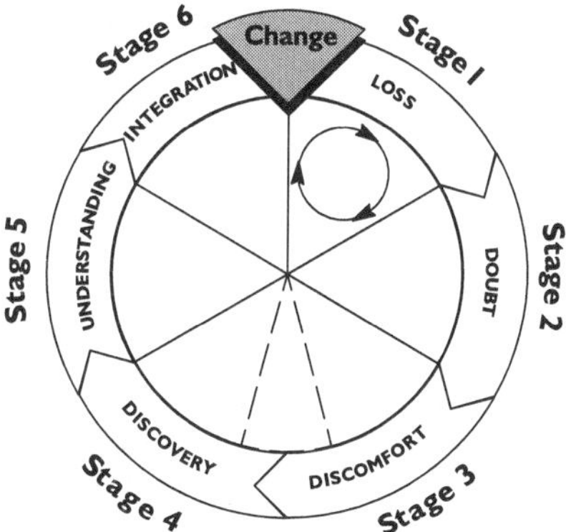

Being Stuck In A Stage

Some people consider the first three stages, Loss, Doubt and Discomfort, as "bad" or negative. Certainly they are rarely a barrel of fun, but they are a reality and provide the foundation pieces to completing the change puzzle. Remember, that there are good and bad aspects of each Stage. When you use the skills that support you in moving through those first three Stages, the experience of the resources, creating safety, gathering information and being motivated, outweighs the stresses you undergo in completing the Stages. There is a tendency to think that getting stuck is only a problem in the first three Stages, but beware! The last three Stages can be even more alluring and tricky. Let's look at examples of the consequences of being stuck in any of the six Stages.

Stage 1: Loss

Battered women or victims of domestic violence often remain stuck in the fear, paralysis, and lack of safety which characterize Stage 1. Continually looping around in this Stage creates a spiral which makes it almost impossible for them to realize that by choosing other options, they can start to create a safe place for themselves. Of course, they often feel as if they have no options, so they take no action. That's why many women who have been victims of domestic violence stay in abusive relationships or continually repeat the same abusive relationship patterns with other partners. Though this seems like an extreme example, it vividly illustrates the consequences of becoming trapped in Stage 1.

Stage 2: Doubt

Choose any current, significant social issue and Stage 2 will be obvious. Usually it makes the news when individuals or groups involved with the issue repeatedly, and with great passion, display the emotional, behavioral, and mental characteristics of Stage 2—resistance, resentment, and skepticism. Some examples of this include: the national health care program, gays in the military, prayer in schools, and of course, abortion. Abortion is one social issue which could forever remain in Stage 2. If people on both sides of the issue could progress to Stage 4, Discovery, they would probably find that they have common ground after all. Maybe then they would have some willingness to resolve their differences and understand their likenesses. You can see, however, that Stage 2 would never allow acknowledgment or agreement. An unwillingness to gather or acknowledge accurate information is the root of all prejudice. The consequences are violence, close-mindedness, hatred, win/lose situations, gridlock and lack of reconciliation.

Stage 3: Discomfort

In America today, hundreds of thousands of men and women suffer from depression severe enough to require medication. The effects of continual bouts of anxiety, combined with low productivity, stress and confusion produce their depression. Those who break through the negative thoughts, feelings, and behaviors of Stage 3 regain their self-esteem and momentum. Unfortunately, stagnation in Stage 3 leaves millions of people unwilling to adapt to the many changes which flood their lives every day. The sad statistics about the number of people with dangerous levels of stress and depression should be motivation enough to move to Stage 4.

Stage 4: Discovery

Frequently "teams" which operate in the workplace get stuck in Stage 4. The teams come up with new solutions and new ideas and are excited by all of the possibilities. They become stuck because they fail to make choices and decisions or take the next step to implement their ideas. Unfortunately, this common problem can undermine the validity and value of what teams bring to an organization. It produces discouraged employees who may be skeptical the next time a team effort is tried.

Many politicians get stuck in Stage 4. These are the ones who empathize with each group of constituents and have a very hard time making or promoting any change that might cause upset or discomfort for anyone. Obviously, this behavior stagnates the change process (in government, this is called grid lock) and eventually, with any luck, ends their political career.

Stage 5: Understanding

The world would be a thinner and healthier place if we could keep dieters from getting stuck in Stage 5. Many people enter weight reduction programs, follow their diet instructions, lose weight, and successfully move to Stage 5, where they feel a new pride and confidence about their accomplishment. The problem is that their sense of pride over the lost weight disguises the need for the dieter to maintain the new healthy eating habits they have acquired. Getting stuck in Stage 5 causes them to go back to the old eating patterns and problems they had before. Being stuck in Stage 5, they have not yet learned how to integrate eating regular food, ordering in restaurants, or going without support group sessions into their change. This is no fault of either the dieter or the program. The point is, that even when someone feels at the peak of the features and benefits of losing weight, he/she must progress to Stage 6 in order to stabilize and integrate the benefits. There are many frustrated dieters who have gained back every ounce they lost because they stopped managing the change by moving on to the next Stage. When they saw the results they didn't move on to stabilizing the new habits that got them there.

Stage 6: Integration

In the 1992 Presidential campaign, President Bush gave us a picture-perfect example of being stuck in Stage 6. At the beginning of the campaign, his popularity had never been higher. He had every reason to believe he was going to be re-elected. George Bush seemingly did not think it was necessary to talk with the voters. He waited too long to appoint someone to plan and run his campaign and he appeared to have misjudged the concerns of the American people and the major issues of the time that he needed to address. Even before Bill

Clinton and Ross Perot proved to be formidable opponents, George Bush should have entered Stage 1 in response to their challenge, which was the start of a big change from being President to being a Presidential candidate again.

If President Bush had been willing to move out of Stage 6 sooner and become Candidate Bush, the 1992 Presidential elections might have had a different result. George Bush experienced the best and worst of times in Stage 6. He was often hailed for his confidence, competence, and stable leadership. He over-stayed his visit in Stage 6 and that created an appearance of arrogance about change that ultimately led to his defeat.

As you go through changes, notice where in the cycle you tend to consistently get stuck. Once you are aware of the Stage that is most likely to "capture" you, you can better prepare yourself before it happens. No matter what the change issue, we all have places where we tend to get stuck or slowed down. We can either be crippled by it or we can plan and compensate for it. It is a choice!

Pattern 2: Be Prepared For Multiple Changes

Be aware that there are always several changes going on at once. To allow all of your changes to form a group creates a mass of continuous fear, confusion, and inappropriate responses and reactions. Each change must be dealt with separately, otherwise, it is difficult to make sense of anything that is going on inside and around you. Of course, every change brings its friends. When it rains, it pours. Multiple changes are the norm. The following story can add some clarity.

Paul has been given a promotion and transferred from Cincinnati to Denver. He is very excited and in his enthusiasm to please his new boss, agrees to report to his new job in two weeks.

Paul floats in the front door, hugs his wife, Karen, and announces the big news. She too, is thrilled and excited. So far, so good.

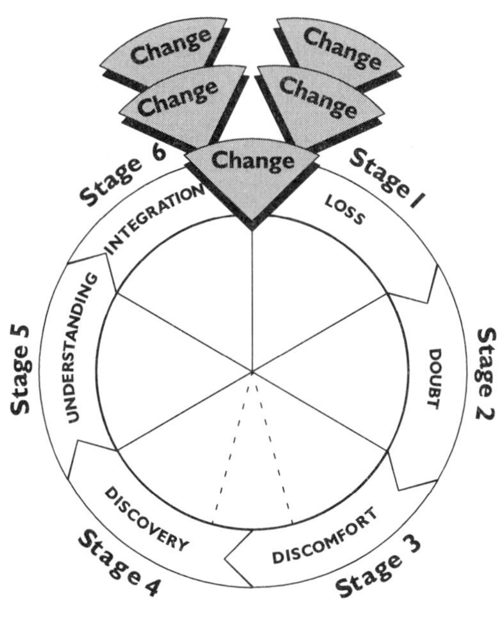

Multiple Changes

Wondering about all the commotion, Sam, their eleven-year-old son walks in and receives the "good news." He is immediately heartbroken. What about his baseball team and his friends? His parents are saddened and begin to "sell" the benefits of moving to Denver. Sam just isn't quite ready to be happy about the move.

Change almost always affects more than one person. Though Paul and Karen seem to be moving quickly and easily through the change, hold off before you make your bets.

Paul and Karen start imagining their new mountain-view home. This is like a dream come true until Paul remembers that the company requires homeowners to make an effort for three months to sell their old house. If, at the end of that time, the house is still unsold, the company policy is to buy it for ninety percent of the market value. Karen feels uncertain about the sale because the market is sluggish and the house needs some cosmetic repair. She realizes they will be very busy getting the home into "For Sale" condition. As she starts to bring up making a plan for the home repairs, Paul has a look of horror on his face and admits that he has agreed to begin the new job in two weeks. Karen is ready to strangle him! Two weeks! What about the repairs, the packing, finding a new house, new schools, etc. Again, change brings change and more change.

You may have had similar experiences. In any change, you will be better prepared to deal with the situation if you keep in mind that it will probably involve other little and not so little changes as well. Mentally and emotionally prepare yourself to deal with all of them.

Always be aware of the other changes that are happening in your life that are unrelated to the initial change, but certainly play into your ability to adapt.

For example, Joe is a young man who received a promotion two months ago and has adjusted well to the change. He has moved to Stage 4, where he is discovering new opportunities and possibilities and using his creativity to find solutions. It's an exciting time. Unfortunately, last week, Joe and his wife, Tina, lost their baby as a result of a very difficult delivery. In that area of his life, Joe is in Stage 2. When talking to Joe, it is evident that he is sad and angry. Unfortunately, he is taking some of his anger out on people at the office. At times, Joe has allowed the changes from his promotion and the loss of his baby to become one.

It is important to identify where you are in the Change Cycle™ for each individual change. Although it is natural for feelings to overlap, this will help you to be more realistic about what is really going on in your life. More importantly, it will assist you in repeating the behaviors, thoughts, and feelings that are producing positive change results.

Once you identify every change you are experiencing and place it in the Change Cycle™, you will become more clear as to what is required for the successful completion of each of them. *Successful Changers* know how to allow the change that is going more positively to flow over into the change areas that are more difficult. For example, in Joe's case, a *Successful Changer* would use the good feelings and resources experienced at work in dealing with the difficult feelings at home rather than allowing the reverse to happen. This alters the natural tendency to let bad feelings negatively impact everything else that's going on around you and allows you to use the good feelings to your advantage.

Pattern 3: Understand The Cyclical Correlations

Because of their location in the cycle, there is a complementarily, cyclical and reciprocal relationship between Stages 1 and 4, Stages 2 and 5, and Stages 3 and 6.

It is useful to note that if a particular Stage seems to be the hardest or easiest for you, then it would be wise to pay attention to the Stage directly across from it on the Change Cycle™. For instance, if you find that Stage 2 causes you the most trouble (perhaps you even try to avoid it altogether), look at Stage 5; it will likely be the other Stage where you experience the most or least intensity.

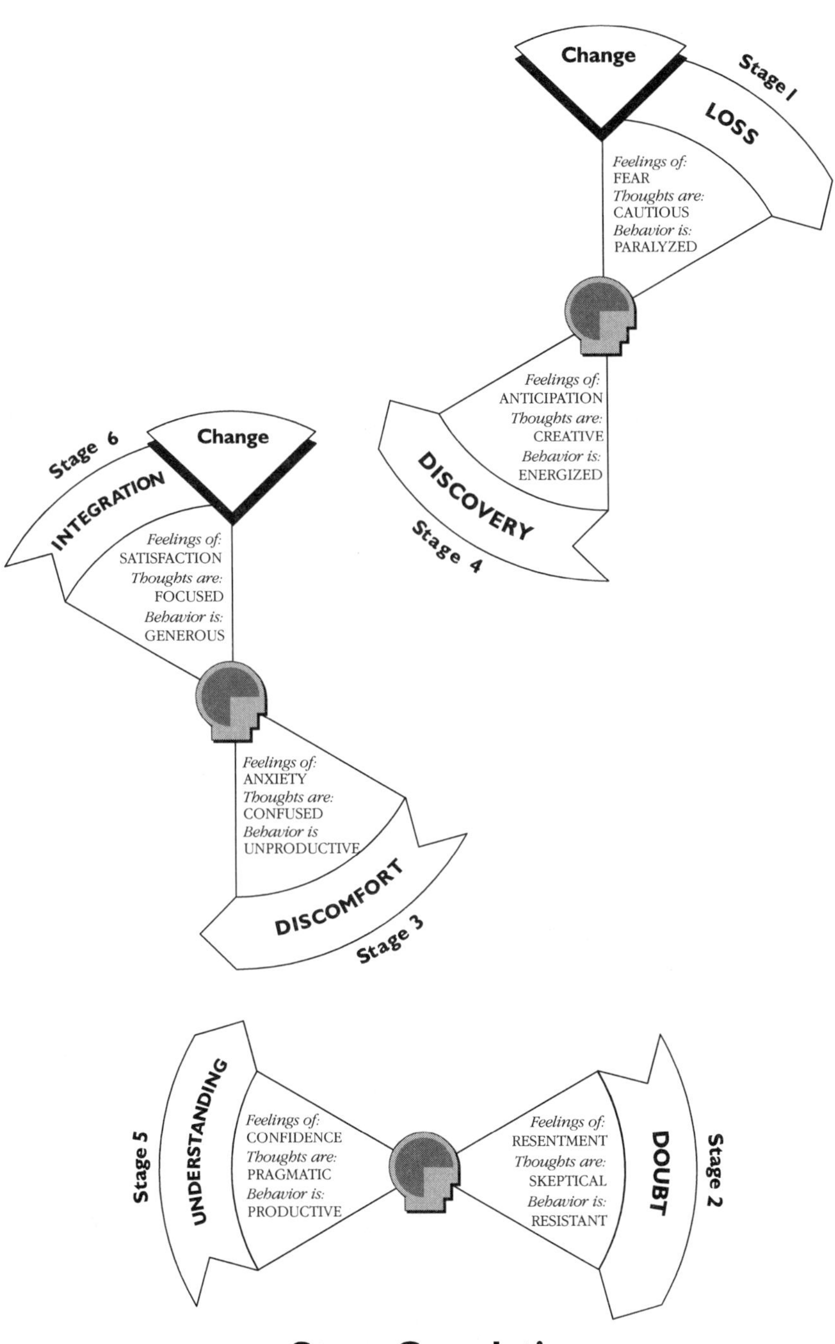

Stage Correlations

If you tend to gravitate toward a particular Stage, identify what you like or what makes you feel competent in that Stage. Also, discern whether, in the complementary Stage, you have the same or opposite skills.

For example, Chris had a good job as the Vice President of Personnel and was well liked by everyone. When it came to people, her skills were far above average. When it came to change, her approach was similar to most people's; haphazard and often misguided.

Chris' main trap was Stage 1. It was her most intensely difficult Stage, while Stage 4 was her strongest. This is a very common pattern. In Stage 1, Chris tended to focus on self-protection, fearing what might happen and what people might think of her. Worrying about failure kept her paralyzed and immobile. Because she did not know how to easily achieve the feelings of safety she needed to advance to Stage 2, Chris spent an inordinate amount of time in Stage 1.

In Stage 4, Chris appeared to be at her best. She rode high on the wave of motivation she had achieved in Stage 3, a belief in the merit of the change, and a certainty that further investigation would lead to new discoveries and exciting opportunities. Her enthusiastic attitude gave her co-workers a sense of well-being.

The trap for Chris was that although Stage 4 felt good and let her use her strengths in working with others, eventually her wave productivity dropped. She spent too much time exploring new options and became slow to make the decisions which would allow her to integrate the change process to the next Stage. Just as with Stage 1, Chris spent inordinate amounts of time in Stage 4.

Pinpointing your problem or favorite Stages increases your ability to identify your own strengths and weaknesses and gives you more control over the change process. It helps you to use it to your advantage.

Keep a written log or journal chronicling your specific thoughts, feelings and behaviors, so that it becomes clear which Stages deserve your extra attention. Some criteria to watch for and measure:

- Keep track of the time it takes to go through each Stage.
- Monitor the intensity that you feel with each Stage.
- Log your perceptions of those tools work that best and those you shy away from.

Time, intensity, and perception are very individual. Since you know yourself better than anyone, you'll know instinctively what your patterns are telling you.

Like walking through your home in the dark, knowing where the hazards are keeps you from banging your knees or stubbing your toes. The secret is knowing where they are and how to avoid them.

The truth is that there are very few limitations in life except the ones we place on ourselves. While that may sound idealistic, the Change Cycle™ clearly shows that we can manage change and use it to create a safer, happier, more productive lifestyle.

Our fervent belief is that people everywhere must learn to understand and manage the changes in their lives. We also believe that, if you use the information and tools available to you, you will be able to respond quickly and effectively to all change and initiate new changes that will improve your life. Ultimately, a better world will be created when all of us are able to create positive changes in our lives.

As you remember all that you've learned from this book, allow your mind to explore the areas of your life where you know you want and need to make changes. It will be obvious to use the Change Cycle™ when external changes come along, yet the Change Cycle™ can be equally useful in giving you the power and confidence to initiate personal changes you know you need and want to make.

For a few minutes, pretend that there are endless possibilities and you can choose to create the life you want.

- What would you change about your life now?
- What would you change about yourself?
- What changes would you have to make in order to be the person you want to be?
- When are you going to take the first step?

When it comes right down to it, change defines what life is all about. The very process of living is that of moving from one change to another. One secret to a happy life is to effectively connect our successful changes, in order to build strong bridges to our future. Another secret:

A little change can change a lot.

Appendix

About Interchange International Inc.

Interchange International Inc. has offices in Washington, D.C., Honolulu, Hawaii, and Durban, South Africa. We provide cutting-edge products and strategies for personal change in corporate and public seminar settings.

We believe that ***personal change precedes organizational change***. As a result of that belief, we have committed ourselves to providing a professional staff of speakers and trainers who can assist you and the people of your organization to master the necessary skills to succeed and prosper in changing environments.

To learn to deal with change in a productive way, call us now. We can help you to . . . Succeed on Purpose!!

INTERCHANGE

KEYNOTES • TRAINING • CONSULTING

WASHINGTON, D.C.

1001 G Street, NW
Suite 200 East
Washington, D.C. 20001-4545
Tel. 202..783..7700
Tel. 800..878..8422
Fax 202..783..7730
Email: changecycl@aol.com
Website: www.changecycle.com

The Secret To Getting Through Life's Difficult Changes

By Lillie R. Brock & Mary Ann Salerno

For ordering and pricing information, call

800..878..8422 or Fax: 202..783..7730

www.changecycle.com

WARNING!!!

Surprisingly, there is no federal law against loaning beloved literary works of art or reading material of any kind to your friends, or worse yet, your family members. It is risky business and you should know the #1 inherent danger of lending this or any book out—you will probably never see it again. Save a relationship and order them their own copy.

Where Are You Successful Changers?

If you are a *Successful Changer* or if you know people who are *Successful Changers*, please write or fax and tell us their story. We hope to use these stories in another book about *Successful Changers*.

If you have an experience about successful change in your own life, we would also like to hear about that.

INTERCHANGE INTERNATIONAL INC.

1001 G Street NW, Suite 200 East

Washington, DC 20001-4545

202..783..7700 800..878..8422

Fax 202..783.7730

Email: changecycl@aol.com

Website: www.changecycle.com

INTERCHANGE

Index

C

D

E

F

G

H

I

K

L

M

O

P

R

S

Love Changes Everything